11 H

The Spirit of Colors

The Art of of Karl Gerstner

Nine Picture Chapters
and Selected Essays

Edited   *by Henri Stierlin*

Translated from the German   by Dennis Q. Stephenson

Foreword   **by Grace Glueck**

Contributions   by François Fricker and
Max Lüscher

The MIT Press
Cambridge, Massachusetts
and London, England

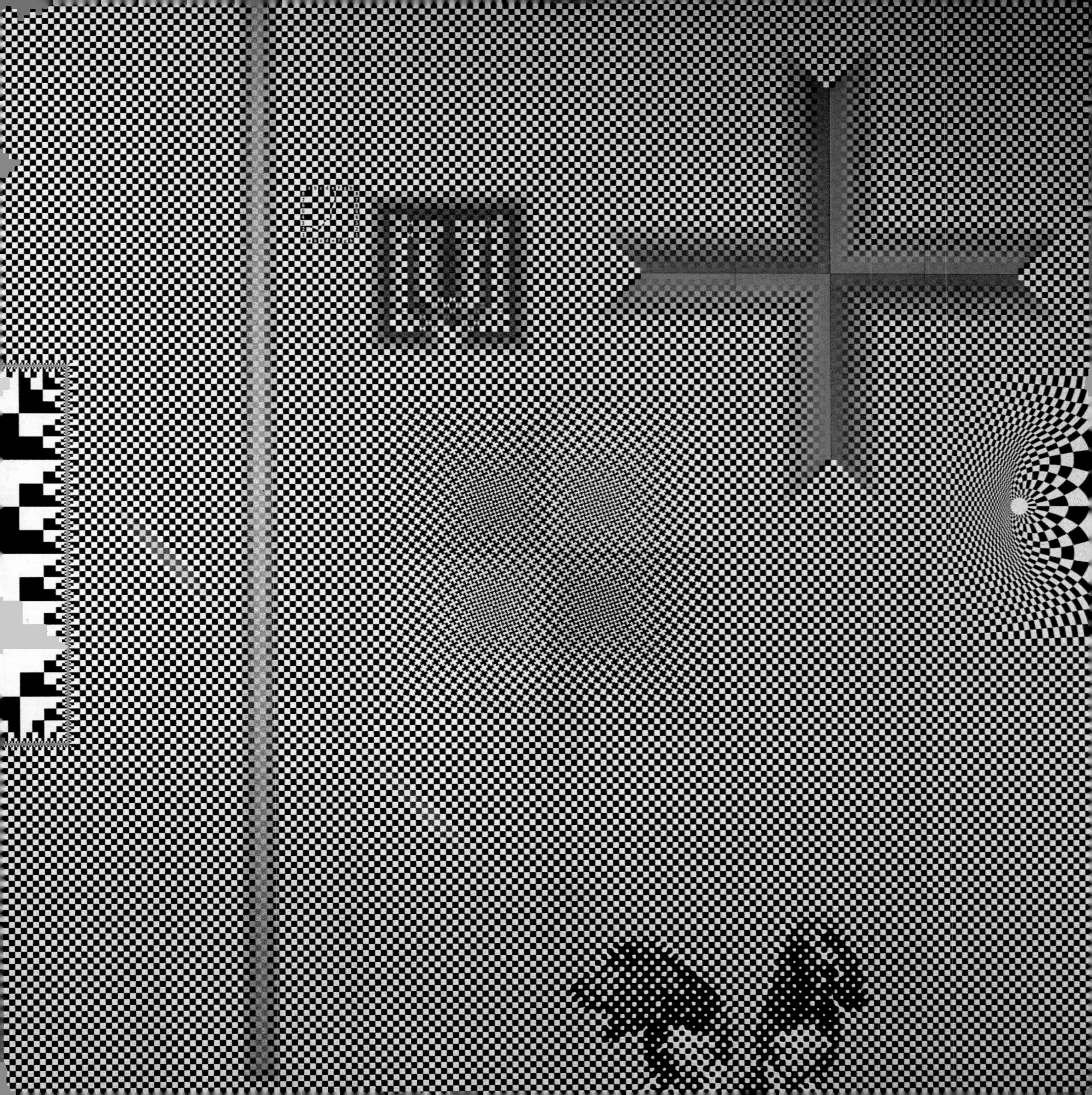
a b c d e f g h
8 7 6 5 4 3 2 1

Photographs	Christian Baur, Basel
	Reto Bernhardt, Basel
	Leonardo Bezzola, Bätterkinden
	Ernst Fieth, Basel
	Walter Grunder, Binningen
	Alex von Steiger, Basel
Separations	Sturm AG, Muttenz
Typesetting and printing	Imprimeries Réunies, Lausanne
Binding	Max Grollimund, Reinach
German edition	*Der Geist der Farbe*
	Karl Gerstner und seine Kunst
	Deutsche Verlags-Anstalt GmbH, Stuttgart
French edition	*L'Esprit des Couleurs*
	L'Art de Karl Gerstner
	Bibliothèque des Arts, Paris
	Editions Sigma, Geneva
Produced by	Editions Sigma
	Printed in Switzerland
© 1981 by	The Massachusetts Institute of Technology

Library of Congress
catalog card number: 81-82618
ISBN 0-262-07084-7

Perceiving Karl Gerstner

by Grace Glueck

Karl Gerstner is a man possessed by color. With a scholar's passion for inquiry, he has devoted nearly 30 years to exploring the properties of this vast but elusive phenomenon of which, like the weather, we all have opinions but limited understanding. And with an artist's gift for exposition, he conveys his findings to us through structures so clearly orchestrated that on seeing them, we can virtually catch color in the very act of invading our sensual apparatus.

"My medium is color, and my theme is what I call the precision of sensation," says Gerstner, a warm and enthusiastic man whose zest for his work is all of a piece with his robust appetite for the feeling side of life. "I'm interested in how colors react on our emotions, our souls. The reality of color and the conscious experience of its effects is what I'm after." His favorite work is his "Color Dome," done between 1974 and 1978 (see page 177), an intimate environment in which the viewer can experience the psychic as well as the physical presence of color, by means of a vibrant spectrum that surrounds him. His model for the "Color Dome," Gerstner explains, was Monet's "Nymphaea" room at the Museum of Modern Art in Paris. "When you are looking at pictures conventionally hung in a museum, you can pass them by. But in this room, you can't escape. The physical presence of color provides an intense emotional experience, in which you can actually feel how color works on you."

Gerstner's intellectual/intuitive approach to his subject draws on a body of color ideas that goes back to the Egyptians and the Assyrians, and includes such wide-ranging sources as Aristotle, the alchemists, Goethe, the contemporary Swiss color psychologist Max Lüscher and the German-Canadian mathematician Günter Wyszecki, known for his scientific/mathematical approach to the perception of colors. Through his goal of exploring the very core of color, Gerstner was led inevitably to a kind of mathematical thinking about it, and although he is not gifted as a mathematician himself, he often bases his works on mathematical theories and speculations. Yet, mathematical thinking is not a goal in itself, he points out; it is an aid to ultimate mastery of one's medium.

Gerstner's "Aperspectives" of the early 1950s, for example (see page 62), which he considers his first real works, derive from Einstein's theory that the universe is, paradoxically, at once finite and endless. "It was a new concept, a new model of space, and I wanted to take it literally. While Cubist paintings reflected new thinking about space and time, they used old media and images–paint, canvas, and the shapes of violins and faces. I felt they hadn't taken the idea as far as it could go."

The "Aperspective" series (Gerstner tends to work in series, over many years, and this is the only one that he has ended) thus had as its aim the creation of a picture that was finite within its borders, but also endless. Each "Aperspective" consists of an arrangement on a plane surface, whose elements can be moved to form new constellations that express the concept of endlessness and endless variations. "A work of art, like a mathematical formula, should be a truth in its own right, a piece of the absolute," Gerstner says. "What counts is its originality, its ability to contain its *raison d'être* in itself. Whether it is considered good or bad, important or unimportant, doesn't interest me. Those qualities only history can judge."

The "Aperspectives" also satisfy a Gerstner ambition of having the viewer participate in the art process. And they tie in with his deeply-held belief in the primacy of principle over execution since, with its endlessly variable components, the picture never comes to rest in a "completed" form. "As Einstein said, what is constant is the formula; the components are interchangeable. Every component is related to every other one, so there's no need for the picture to be 'fixed'."

By producing such works as these, Gerstner was already moving away from the traditional concept of art as a "unique" endeavor, in which "the moment and the mood" are captured. In making an object that was "conceptual and repeatable," he was declaring his "objectivity" in relation to the "subjectivity" of, say, the Abstract Expressionists. "Much as I admire Jackson Pollock," he notes, "I couldn't work in that way, because I couldn't imagine that anyone would be interested in any of my spontaneous moods and impressions." In contrast to an art like Pollock's, which places the emphasis on the artist's individual expression, Gerstner sees his work as goal-oriented, going beyond the "subjective". He cites Josef Albers, "who wanted to find out how colors act and react, and so treated a subject of general interest that had nothing to do with his mood or biography. There has always been through the history of art," Gerstner muses, "this kind of division: classic, a direction toward objectivity, generalization; vs. romantic, meaning the personal, the spontaneous. I'd put myself on the side of the classical, though there are many contradictions."

One is always struck by the elegant and impeccable craftsmanship of Gerstner's work, a Bauhaus kind of perfection that is not only geared to please our esthetic sensibilities, but is also aimed at making an adequate presentation of a concept. "If you have a precise idea of what you want, it's only possible to execute it precisely," he says. Most of his paintings, for example, are done in layers, stepped arrangements whereby each color is separated from the next, so that the works appear as reliefs rather than flat surfaces. "The idea is not to put one color side by side with another one, as in conventional paintings," Gerstner says, "I want to make it clear that color is materially the form itself, not just the surface of the form."

At once a dreamer and an intensely practical *metteur-en-scène*, Gerstner brings his ideas to realization in a refurbished sawmill that stands on the river Ill in the bucolic Alsatian countryside near his native city of Basel. In the studio of his "mill," designed by the artist himself, he works with meticulous methodology on all aspects of his production, from standardizing his color formulae to spray-painting and glueing the actual objects. So carefully arranged are the neat boxes of precisely-graded color cards, the bottles of pigments (he uses only ten, the "purest and most durable," found after years of research) and the drawers full of painstaking concept sketches that the studio has as much the aspect of a laboratory as the workplace of an artist.

Looking around it, one sees, in varying stages of completion, such Gerstner creations as the "Color Forms" (see page 180), relief constructions in which he investigates the correlation between form and color, the "Color Sounds" (see page 160), square-format works in which, by means of subtle color gradations, he explores the emotional effect of color on the viewer, and drawings for a new series–not discussed in this book–that he considers "objects of an individual mythology." The latter include such larger works as his recent "Planetarian Structure," done for the Luftwaffe high school near Munich, a polychrome sculpture conceived as a "sender of colors to the planets," and–standing on the grounds of the mill–"La Fleur du Mal," a structure whose clusters of blues form a crown around a huge and ominous dark gray stamen. (See page 23). In these objects, representing colors in three dimensions, he sees the further development of his work, the "Tenth chapter," so to speak.

From time to time, he also works on a giant kind of painting-chart that takes up an entire wall of the studio. More or less a map of his personal cosmogony, it has preoccupied him for nearly 30 years, and continually undergoes revision. The painting, called "Genesis," develops from a gray diamond which forms its very center and represents "nothingness, the state before everything." From this "nothingness" develop the first opposites, light and darkness, indicated by black and white. The black-and-white areas are then divided into always smaller parts that proceed toward infinity. In the square that forms this part of the painting, "infinity" is invoked without actually being visible, thanks to a mathematical paradox of Felix Klein.

On the black-and-white checked ground of the picture, other events occur; among them, a pair of Bassett hounds that suggest "innocent beings" involved in creation; a profile of Duchamp, a kind of *spiritus rector* to Gerstner; a cross of red and green that symbolizes "the old mythology of how colors are created from black and white" (described in the essay on Goethe's color theory, see page 42); a computer-generated portrait of Gerstner himself. The description could go on and on, of parts already executed and in prospect. But suffice it to mention that, with Duchampian humor, Gerstner indicates in the upper left corner that the whole universe not yet finished, is already falling apart.

The metaphysical nature of the work may be certified by the fact that every night around midnight, a bat–for which he leaves the window open–flies into the studio and hangs from a lighting track, gazing at "Genesis" for an hour or so before leaving. And early each morning, a raven beats with its beak on a studio window. The artist laughingly attributes these phenomena to the spiritual force generated by the painting. (Poe's "The Raven" is his favorite poem.)

Gerstner's preoccupation with art as a social force goes back to his childhood in Basel, at the start of World War II. He was nine years old then, and he still remembers the atmosphere of the city: the pro and con-Nazi discussions among Swiss citizens, the strong anti-Hitlerism of his parents and their friends, the conscription of fathers and teachers into the military, and the frightening prospect of a German victory.

When the war ended, he was 15, and already showing considerable talent for visual expression. He had experienced so intensely the danger of Hitlerism that he felt it "a moral obligation" to use that talent "toward something constructive for the future." But the education he sought, a Bauhaus kind of training in which "daily life became the practice of art," was not so easily come by in Basel after World War II. The times hardly favored a progressive outlook. "At the end of the war, contrary of what one would expect after the Third Reich's policy toward art, the spirit of art and life was not only conservative, but reactionary," Gerstner recalls. In those years it was the progressives who saved the marvellous medieval city of Basel from being torn down and replaced by speculative, nasty new stuff.

Though Gerstner became involved in these violent disputes, his main ambition was not to conserve, but to look to the future and to contribute to that his energy. Fuelled by the spirit of the Bauhaus–still alive in Zurich, thanks to artists such as Max Bill, a former student at the now-extinct German design school, who was practising simultaneously as an architect, designer, painter and sculptor–Gerstner decided to study typography, one of the graphic arts for which Switzerland was later to become a mecca. With his friends, he began to think in terms of a "democratic culture oriented toward the future, in which art would belong to daily life, and objects belonging to daily life would take on the quality of art. We thought of the Bauhaus not as a theory, a school, but as an agency for practical life. The Bauhaus philosophy meant to us nothing else than doing right whatever had to be done. You must have as much respect for the task of making a spoon as making a picture, though of course making a picture is much more complex. There's only the first decision, is it right to do?"

To realize their ideas, Gerstner and some friends planned a design business to be called "Bureau Basel." Their utopian concept was "a kind of Bauhaus-in-practice that would concern itself not with esoteric theories, but problems of daily life. We wanted to do all kinds of things, from designing visiting cards to city planning." Eventually, the "Bureau" evolved into an advertising agency, founded in 1959 by Gerstner and Markus Kutter. "We did advertising design and publicity, but we weren't the usual kind of agency. We were unconventional and avant-garde. We decided that our contribution would be that we'd make every job we got a piece of art."

The agency, with the addition of Paul Gredinger as a partner, became known as GGK, and is now the largest in Switzerland, with offices in major European cities, as well as New York and São Paulo. But in 1970, bored with administrative details and feeling that the agency's growing devotion to "business as usual" was increasingly subverting its original rationale, Gerstner left the firm to devote full time to his art.

His early orientation toward Bauhaus concepts had led inevitably to an interest in Constructive art, represented in Switzerland by the so-called "concrete artists" such as Bill, Richard Lohse and Camille Graeser. His engagement led him to write a widely-discussed essay, "Cold Art?", published in 1957, analyzing some major works of these artists, going back to the roots of Constructive art in general, and looking toward its future development. "Everyone considered the art 'cold'. I wanted to take this prejudice and analyze it," Gerstner says.

The essay was of crucial importance to his own development as an artist, because in the process of analyzing the work of his "spiritual parents," he clarified what he himself wanted to do. His chief conclusion was that he had to go deeper and more radically into the exploration of colors, because he found a "major contradiction between the conclusive concept of the formal structures made by these artists and their more or less arbitrary use of colors."

"I began to investigate, because I didn't know as much as I wanted to," he says, "and then I became aware that there was a general lack of consciousness in the field of colors. My basic goal was to relate colors in an absolute and distinctive way to a formal structure. Only if this were possible would I be able to reach the goal I was after: making pictures that existed as undeniable truths in themselves."

Another artist who was also aware of the lack of knowledge in the field was Josef Albers, the former Bauhaus teacher who had emigrated to the United States, and who had dedicated himself as an artist/researcher in the phenomenon of color. Seeing and hearing of his work, Gerstner made contact with him, and a friendship developed. As is Gerstner's wont with artists he admires, he became involved with Albers' work (he regards his "Color Sound" series as a sort of homage to Albers' endless "Homage to the Square" motifs), making it at the same time a departure point for his own interests. "Albers was one of the first to explore colors in a precise and rational way, describing them as phenomena with an intriguing life of interactions," he says. "But I became interested in the *effects* of the phenomena."

There were many other artists in whose work Gerstner was interested, and from whose investigations he profited. After the Albers connection, he discovered Robert Strübin, a Swiss artist who went about systematically transforming music into a concrete art, Hans Hinterreiter, another Swiss artist, living, still unknown, in Ibiza and carrying out a rich and original oeuvre, and Jakob Weder, who calculates his thousands and thousands of different color shades with the aid of a Hewlett-Packard calculator. And yet, as much from those artists whose interests and attitudes are similar to his own, Gerstner has benefited from others of "opposite head," such as Dieter Rot, André Thomkins and Daniel Spoerri, with whom he once joined in an exhibition called "The Friends." In his appartment in Basel, different rooms are devoted to the work of these and others he admires, including the late Mauritius Escher, the Dutch printmaker whose topsy-turvy world view appeals to the cosmologist in Gerstner.

Though the work of some of these artists seems a long way indeed from Gerstner's own impeccable renditions, he explains that the similarities are in the end more fundamental than the differences. Take, for example, the oeuvre of Spoerri, as physically "messy" as Gerstner's is "clean." Among the more prominent Spoerri works in the Gerstner collection are a series of impromptu tables bearing the results of meals, which Spoerri has fixed permanently.

What attracted him to Spoerri's work, Gerstner explains, is that "it's an art of ideas, like my own. He finds a situation and without changing it, he 'fixes' it. His conception of art is that he chooses total chance, whereas I choose total construction. In either case, one's aesthetic involvement is only a question of getting accustomed to it. After all, Duchamp, an artist who's meant much to me, declared a urinal an art work, and it immediately went into a museum."

Though Gerstner does not lack for recognition in the world of art, he is a prophet without honor in his native Basel, where he reached the age of 40 before having his first local show. But he preserves a calm ambivalence toward the situation. "Sometimes I'm sad about it, but on the whole it's been very good—it's kept me going in my own direction. If I'd been in Paris, I might have had more recognition, but at the same time been more damaged."

But because Basel is a comfortable city to work in, he stays on, continuing to look to the future. "Since childhood, I've been very much aware that the time I had to live grew shorter with each day. At 30, I consulted an insurance company for a probability calculation on the rest of my days. I figured out the time left, and I conceived a lifelong calendar. You'd be astonished how few the days are!" he says, ebulliently.

Annotated Biography

STRENGER (= more strict): anagram of GERSTNER. By adding the first name KARL, André Thomkins extended this to STRENG, KLARER (= strict, clearer).

* * *

André Thomkins also created the palindrome "ART, SI GERSTNER APPARENTS REGISTRA" = Art, if Gerstner will register what appears. Which Thomkins interprets to mean: He raises appearances which he systematically registers to the status of art.

* * *

Born in Basel, 1930. Cancer. His horoscope is unusual and unusually propitious. The sun is in the house of happiness and harmony. The conjunction of Uranus and Venus predestines him to be an artist. His weakness is to be locked in controversy, struggle, and dramatic conflicts.

* * *

In response to Serge Stauffer's question, "What is your capital fault?," he replied: "I overrate my importance"–in the light of which all that follows below must be seen.

* * *

When he was ten years old, he went to the *Gymnasium* in Basel. At this time he wanted to become a chemist. But he became something else: instead of chemical he produced optical syntheses. As a trained typographer and–at the same time–as an untrained maker of pictures.

When he was twenty, he set up on his own–with the aim of putting into practice, to the best of his ability, the Bauhaus philosophy of the unity of culture. As a typographer he sought to design the things of everyday life like works of art; and as a maker of pictures to design works of art like the things of everyday life.

* * *

When he was thirty, he and Markus Kutter opened an office for "advertising, graphic design and publicity," which in the course of time added Paul Gredinger and about 250 others to its number and grew to be the GGK advertising agency: Basel, Düsseldorf, Milan, Paris, Vienna, São Paulo, New York.

* * *

When he was forty, he retired from the agency. For one thing, he realized that the Bauhaus philosophy led to many contradictions. But he also wanted to concentrate on what had always been close to his heart: doing nothing, having time, and making pictures.

* * *

1

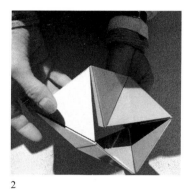

2

18

3

Two examples from his agency work, as an illustration of a mischievous notion: to create art where nobody expects it.

A kinetic light sculpture for "Birra Prinz Bräu," about 100 feet long and 20 feet high, was for years a prominent feature in the station square at Milan (Figure 1).

A kinetic object–a Möbius band of colored triangles–served the Burda corporation as an emblem (Figure 2).

* * *

Until he left the agency he developed his artistic ideas side by side with his business, with the two sometimes intersecting. For example, in the question: how do pictures ever get to the public at all?

One answer was to deal with pictures as if they were a commodity; that is to say, first, offer them where all such commodities are to be had: in stores; second, produce pictures in large numbers; third, compensate for the loss of originality by making each picture alterable, and alterable in a million times more ways than the total edition of pictures; fourth, leave the altering to the consumer, who not only makes his own original but as many of them as he pleases.

* * *

What lay in his power–to design this type of picture and to propose it as a prototype for the purpose envisaged–he executed from 1952 onward; see Chapter 1, Aperspectives, page 62.

* * *

Another answer was the Poster Art Scheme: a museum in the street which he initiated in Zurich in 1961. Pictures by Bill, Graeser, Lohse, Loewensberg, Wyss, and himself were printed as posters; each was exhibited for two weeks at 500 sites at a time; each signed. Figure 3 shows his contribution.

* * *

This same chapter should also record the revival of Edition MAT, 1963, after its founder Daniel Spoerri had given it up.

In 1964 and 1965 he edited two new collections jointly with Daniel Spoerri. Under the new program, Originals in Series, each contained twelve objects from all contemporary trends; from Albers, Arman, Arp, Baj, Boriani, Bury, Christo via Lichtenstein to Soto, Tinguely, Villeglé. The publisher was Hein Stünke, Cologne.

In 1965 he also published–again jointly with Daniel Spoerri–the Edition MAT MOT; literature and art in "black boxes;" with contributions from, among others, Brecht, Filliou, Thomkins, Rot, Williams.

In connection with the Edition MAT he wrote an essay, "How Much May Art Cost?" (published in the catalog to the exhibition "ars multiplicata," Cologne, 1968).

* * *

As a gesture of social commitment he organized an exhibition in the windows of the Kaufhof store in Dortmund, 1969. As part of this an object was distributed as a give-away: the Kinetic Spiral, with which the public could produce all kinds of individual emblems (Figure 4).

* * *

4

In 1973 Herbert Distel invited him to design a work of art on a page of a newspaper (the Basel *National-Zeitung*), which he did by converting it into an invitation to the public to make their own art (Figure 5).

* * *

He likes to reflect on what he does. His first written work on art was for *Spirale* No. 5: the description of one of his alterable pictures, including ideological position (see page 66).

* * *

Immediately thereafter he wrote his first book, which appeared in 1957: *Cold Art?*, an analysis of the development and status of a form of painting committed not to mathematics but rather to mathematical thinking, meaning: logic in art.

* * *

In 1963 he published *Designing Programmes*. The book went through several editions, including English, Spanish, and Japanese versions. It contains a collection of essays that account for its program: instead of solutions for problems, programs for solutions.

He brought this basic idea to the notice of a wider public in an exhibition at the Museum of Modern Art, New York, 1973. The catalog to this exhibition, "Think Program," summarizes the methodology and extends it into philosophy.

* * *

When it became apparent that his ideas of a social do-it-yourself art were idealistic and hence unrealizable, he wrote in 1970 a breviary, *Do-It-Yourself Art*; a sporadic but extensive collection of modern techniques of inspiration.

* * *

5

19

In 1978 Pablo Stähli published *Color Lines–24 Facsimile Pages from a Sketchbook*, with a text on the personality of Andreas Speiser, to whom Gerstner is greatly indebted as a mentor.

* * *

Although the manuscript of another book–"Review of My Failures"–has been completed, it will not be published. The reader would find it mainly an account of the uselessness of his efforts to persuade the public to realize new ideas in art.

* * *

Among other things it would mention a kinetic object–the 82-foot Color-Time Pylon–which he designed in 1965 for the German Television Corporation, Cologne.

Or a project for the Ruhr University at Bochum. What is typical about this is its ostensible untypicality: it is an environment in which sun, wind, and water are collaborators.

All these projects–the Theater Square in Basel is another–are not conceived as "art in architecture." Rather, they are the mise-en-scènes of squares, free spaces in the town, the countryside; not a memorial either for the artist or for a potentate, but environments–atmospheric intensive-care units for the people who live there.

* * *

And now there is this book, which owes its existence to the indefatigable initiative of Henri Stierlin.

It contains all the important sections, "chapters," of his work. As a supplement, mention might be made here of a few works which originated on special occasions which do not fall within these chapters.

* * *

For example, the Homage to Marcel Duchamp: "Monsieur Marcel Duchamp et Madame Rose Sélavy mis à nu, descendant un escalier, même."

The king and the queen are stepping down a tiered chessboard which grows increasingly flat, increasingly gray. Both are lathed, with the profile of Duchamp. Their shadow is fixed, because it will no longer fade away. If 25 cents is inserted, the pair rotate in the manner of the Roto-reliefs to simulate vertical movement: the king upward, the queen downward. The money was intended for the chess player Caissa, for whose benefit Duchamp organized an exhibition in New York, 1969 (Figure 6).

* * *

7

For the "Eat Art" of Daniel Spoerri he designed in 1970 the Taste Perceptor. An object of 17 graded essences–from sweet to sour, from bitter to salty; at the point of intersection the quintessence. It was a conversion (and a persiflage) of the optical series into the gustatory domain (Figure 7).

* * *

His affinity for the elements of Nature found concrete form in an object that was created for a sad occasion: in the Aeolian harp for his friend Hans Tanner, who died in 1967 (Figure 8).

* * *

Mention remains to be made of another picture of (for him) colossal dimensions–20 feet by 10 feet–on which he has been working (or not as the case may be) for 25 years. He calls it "Grand'œuvre." The allusion to the alchemists is not fortuitous; its title is "Genesis." On the simplest possible basic structure of a black-white square grid (the grid units each of 15 mm) some 50 "events" take place, all of them both moving outside the grid and also returning to it (see pages 6/7).

* * *

The only happening he ever organized took place without a public: the burning of about eighty Color Sounds, which, because of a material defect, did not measure up to his requirements. It was the violent end to an experience which was in many ways painful (Figure 9).

* * *

His first exhibition was held early in 1957: at the Club Bel Etage, Zurich, he showed serial and alterable objects which met with amiable astonishment. The critics asked–as they continued to do for many years to come–whether that was really art?

Since the 1960s he has been regularly represented by Denise René and/or Hans Mayer. There were exhibitions first of all (1962) in Paris, then in Esslingen, Krefeld, and by turns in Düsseldorf (1969/71/72/74/78), Paris (1967/71/73/75) and New York (1973/75).

* * *

In addition he has exhibited in, among other cities, Cologne at the Galerie Der Spiegel (1963/65), New York at George Staempfli (1965/67), Amsterdam at Rikjie Swart (1970), Genoa at the Cooperativa Boccadasse (1966), Tokyo at the Tokyo Gallery (1966).

More recently he has shown work at Marcel Liatowitsch in Basel, at the Galerie arte/contacto in Caracas, at Jörg Janisch in Munich, at Josef Müller-Brockmann at

8

9

21

Rapperswil, at Brigite Lopes in Zurich, at Franco Bombelli in Cadaques.

* * *

He has taken part in numerous group exhibitions, as in "Konkrete Kunst," Zurich (1960); "Neue Tendenzen," Zagreb (1961/63) and Paris (1964); "The Responsive Eye," New York (1965); "Documenta 4," Kassel (1968); "Environment," Utrecht (1968); "Today's Half Century," Buffalo (1968); "Düsseldorfer Art Scene," Edinburgh (1970); "Kunst, was ist das?," Hamburg (1979).

* * *

His most cherished memory of all is the exhibition "Freunde, Fruend, Friends," with Diter Rot, Daniel Spoerri, André Thomkins. And many friends of friends, with Dorothy Iannone, George Brecht, Robert Filliou, 1969, in the Kunsthallen in Bern and Düsseldorf.

* * *

Museums have also shown surveys of his work. First, in 1969, the Karl-Ernst-Osthaus-Museum, Hagen; in 1974, the Museum of Fine Arts, Düsseldorf (in Friedrich Heckmann's series "Prinzip seriell"); in 1978, the Moderne Galerie, Bottrop; in 1978, the Museum of Fine Arts, Solothurn. He has particularly pleasant memories of this last exhibition–because of the devoted care given by André Kamber, which has been reflected in a meticulously prepared catalog.

* * *

Actually he is an inveterate loner, a nonconformist–which label (if any at all) he likes best. Nevertheless he allowed himself to be elected president of a registered society: *Das Internationale Künstlergremium* (the International Artists Association, with headquarters in Cologne).

What interested him was the extension of the "friends" idea onto a general plane: to discover the common element among so many different artists as Josef Beuys, Heinz Mack, Klaus Rinke, and some hundred other members of the Association. In 1979 he handed the task over to Dietrich Helms, after organizing two symposiums in Basel and Berlin; theme: Art is not made by Ministers of Cultural Affairs.

* * *

In 1976 he converted a ruined sawmill in Alsace into a studio, the sunny side of which appears in the photograph along with the sculpture "La Fleur du Mal."

Is Constructive Art
at an End?
Or at Its Beginning?

24

The Constructives "are like pedantic and puritanical hygienists who go through the drill of geometrical mathematics with the calculatory exactitude of petty bookkeepers." This sentence on page 129 struck me like a bolt from the blue.

First, the author of the book I was reading had up to this point–and in general–shown a sympathetic interest in constructive art. Second, he cited as evidence an essay of mine ("Cold Art?") in which I had attempted to prove the contrary. The author was Konrad Farner; the book, *Der Aufstand der Abstrakt-Konkreten* (Neuwied, 1970).

I was puzzled, wrote to Konrad Farner–it was shortly before his death–and received the following reply: he would not entirely rule out the possibility that in the remote future the glass-bead game of constructive art may find a place in society. But today was not the time for it. I had to realize (he said) that there were more urgent problems for us to deal with.

* * *

**The Artist
as the Spirit of the Age?**

Konrad Farner's point of view is certainly worth considering–and is in general widely held. That is why I am writing here the reply which I never got round to writing to him.

Has an artist ever had time to seek an age for himself? Should he abstain from doing what he feels to be fit and proper and what his talents fit him for because the time is not right?

I would have reminded Farner the historian of the situation in Italy shortly before 1500. In Rome Cesare Borgia, the son of a pope and a fratricide, became a cardinal. The Medici were driven out of Florence, the fanatic Savonarola held the populace in thrall with his penitential homilies. Botticelli burned his worldly and therefore sinful pictures. And what was worse, he stopped painting. A little later Savonarola was burned at the stake. All the great families and the city states formed changing coalitions with one another and were at the same time embroiled in a quarrel with a French king.

In short, social conditions can hardly be imagined more chaotic. Or the art created at the same time more grandiose.

Perugino, Signorelli, Ghirlandaio, Mantegna, the younger Bellini, and Giorgione were at work. Michelangelo was creating the *Pietà*, Leonardo da Vinci the *Last Supper*. Memories of Piero della Francesca were still alive. And Raphael was beginning to show his mastery.

True, there are great artists who have devoted their art to the service of a cause. Picasso and his *Guernica* come to mind most readily. But there will come a time when only a few will recall the event which is the subject of the picture. Just as there are few people nowadays who can still detect in *Gulliver's Travels* the caustic criticism of an English past.

A great work of art is not great because of the social criticism it embodies. Rather it is great in spite of it: because it transcends such criticism and the passage of time and makes its impact here and now. This certainly does not mean that an artist is under no obligation to concern himself with the society in which he lives. I take that to be self-evident–and I expect others to do so as well.

No, I cannot see that constructive art has no justification today.

       * * *

This has all ignored the fact that there has hardly ever been a movement which has come to grips with the problems of its time with such notable–not to say missionary–zeal as the Russian Constructivists and the Dutch Neoplasticists–as the word *constructive* implies.

**The Artist
as Missionary?**

The ardor and conviction of the artists did not meet with any particular response from the public. In Russia the former were regarded as *bourgeois* and decadent, in the West the latter were pilloried as bolshevistic and revolutionary.

Down to the present, constructive art has remained art for a minority of the minority of those who are interested in art. Its incubation period is longer than that of any other variety of art–but then its ultimate impact is obviously all the more forceful.

All the founding fathers have achieved recognition only after their death, but today it is extremely difficult–and therefore a costly business–to obtain a picture by, say, Mondrian. Two years ago a work by Malevich changed hands for almost four million Swiss francs–making it one of the most expensive in modern art.

If the aspirations of the pioneers did not evoke the desired response from the public, it was not–or not exclusively–the public's fault. Konrad Farner's explanation is that the general validity of our art, which was categorically demanded by the psychologizing, philosophizing, and sociologizing patristic teachers–Mondrian, Gabo, Moholy, Bill–got largely bogged down in the uniquely subjective. Our "religious atheism" (he wrote) manifests itself in a symbolism of colors and surfaces, a symbolism of lines or numbers as mysticism. And the mystic is the greatest of all individualists, the most asocial of all believers.

Perhaps we should say that great constructive art was not great because of its missionary elements. But rather in spite of them. True, Mondrian was in his heart of hearts a mystic rather than a missionary. It is no mere chance that in his early years he bore the stamp of a theosophy of Netherlands provenience.

That precisely the pictures of a mystic, even a modern one, should (because of their straight lines and primary colors) look so utterly rational–that is what is hard to see.

* * *

The Artist as Constructor?

What makes the approach to constructive art difficult is its closeness–real or alleged–to geometry, or worse still (because more abstract) to mathematics. Art and mathematics are like fire and water. The water of numbers extinguishes the fire of sensations.

It is generally held, writes the mathematician Andreas Speiser, that "a formula is something dead and that only immediate sensation is alive. But formula and sensation are not opposites. Rather, the former is a necessary complement to the latter. Everyone has a continuous flux of feelings and sensations, but in most cases they leave not a trace behind. Only through the formula do they acquire a lasting content; without calculation everything is swept away by the wind."

The most convincing proof of Speiser's contention is to be found precisely where one would least expect to find it: among the Romantics. In Friedrich Schlegel's writings (the "Athenäums-Fragmenten") we read: "It is obvious that it would be premature to call poetry or prose art before they have reached the point where they construct their works from beginning to end" (please read this sentence again).

The philosopher's demand is satisfied in the work of the poet; we can check this by reading Edgar Allan Poe's description of how he constructed "The Raven" with relentless precision, in order to evoke the most romantic feelings. Compared with him we constructives of the twentieth century are harmless amateurs.

"True mathematics," wrote Poe's predecessor Novalis, "is the actual instrument of magic; the highest life is mathematics; the life of the gods is mathematics; pure mathematics is religion."

In art the constructive is a category as old as art itself. But in contradistinction to construction in the art of previous centuries (say, the construction of correct perspective) "constructive art" is something new. It does not represent reality but generates it.

* * *

The picture a reality in its own right–what I have in mind is this: just as the mathematician creates conceptual models which are logically self-contained, the artist must be able to create sensuous models which are logically self-contained.

Logically self-contained means absolute in the sense that a modern scientist, Joachim Otto Fleckenstein, defines: "Even if there is never knowledge of the absolute there is nevertheless absolute knowledge. The domain of this absolute knowledge is mathematics."

To transfer this definition to art is not so extravagant as it may appear. For like the elements of mathematics those of art–forms and colors–are every bit as absolute and determinable as numbers and signs.

* * *

**The Artist
as Mathematician?**

Eins (German: one)–an anagram of *Sein* (German: being)–stands for indivisible unity. And as a dialectical complement to it we have *Nein* (German: no), the negation of one–nil, nonentity. *Zwei* (German: two) is the *Entzweiung* (disunion) of unity, *Verzweiflung* (despair) and *Zweifel* (doubt). With three, so to speak, the dynamic component comes into being: the three dimensions of space (height, breadth, depth); the three dimensions of time (yesterday, today, tomorrow); the three dimensions of the creaturely (birth, life, death).

Not only number but also form says something or nothing–depending on who listens and how. Kandinsky *(On the Spiritual in Art)* gave original meanings a refurbishing. Horizontal and vertical, for example, as symbols of death and life. "The first is lying, the second standing, walking, locomotion, finally climbing to a height. Carrying–growing. Passive–active. Relative: female–male."

The main point is this: an artist draws on archetypal components out of which the contents of consciousness have taken shape. And if he does not get to the bottom of truth, at least he gets nearer to it.

* * *

I can also regard a color–one way or another–as a precise fact (the subject of this book). Or as a kind of archeological adventure, namely, to trace back red in time to the point when there was no name for it.

If red has the same linguistic root as the word *blood*, this means that *blood* also originally denoted the color. And so, whatever blood, the vital fluid, meant to mankind in fact and throughout the myths has gone into the concept of this color. And is still accessible in all its immediacy to the felt response of the senses, even though spilled. And so on. And so on.

This, I hold, is the material out of which constructive pictures are made. And not out of the vacuous forms and colors of the display artist. And not out of the figures of the bookkeeper, dear Konrad Farner.

If–again and again throughout time–it has been the purport of art (also its content) to recall the primal so as to point to the future, then there opens up for constructive art a vast and fertile field of which only one tiny corner has so far been tilled. And if one day there is a harvest, dear Konrad Farner, I too shall be where you are. Perhaps we shall share the celestial fruit together?

(*From* National-Zeitung Basel, *19 January, 1977*.)

28

Conception–Perception

Fifteen Reflections on a Proposition of Max Bill

Max Bill said: *"Art can mediate thinking in such a way that the thought is directly perceptible information."* (Eduard Hüttinger, *Max Bill*; Zurich, 1977)

1

Can we transpose the proposition and say: "Science can mediate sensation in such a way that the sensation becomes directly perceptible information"?

2

Does this imply that sensation and thinking are a pair of opposites; sensation correlated with art, thinking with science? Now, even the most dream-rapt artist needs reflection as well as intuition; vice versa in the case of the scientist.

No thought is possible without sensation, and no sensation without thought, to quote Hermes Trismegistos. And man has a body and a soul. If these two parts concur in sensation, there emerges therefrom–shaped by the intelligence–thought.

3

Art as the opposite of science? Masaccio, who is often hailed as the first painter of modern times, was a member of the guild of apothecaries and grocers.

Even Leonardo objected to his art being classed as a handicraft: "But you [the poets] have put painting among the handicrafts. ... Whereas painting embraces all forms of Nature, you have only the names, which are not so generally understandable as the forms."

4

The conceptual categorization of the world, such as we today take for granted, is a comparatively recent achievement. It is absurd to accept it as final. It calls for retrospective and prospective meditation.

If a flashback to origins can be of value in looking into the future: the Greek word *nous* connotes both reason and feeling, in addition to other meanings–including meaning.

5

What is thinking? I should have thought I would have known.

Descartes and Pascal: near contemporaries, devout Christians, compatriots, philosophers, mathematicians, as thinkers both pronounced skeptics–with so much in common, what a difference! One of them utilizes doubt to prove the effectiveness of thinking, the other to prove its limitations. One, a rationalist by method, thinks discursively; the other, a mystic by conviction, intuitively.

6

What is sensation? Wittgenstein asks: how should I perceive red if I did not have the concept for it available? Should I perceive it at all?

7

Modern anthropologists assume that early man–equipped with the same visual apparatus as ourselves–could not distinguish between colors, but only between light and darkness. Accordingly the perception of colors is not a natural but a cultural achievement. I ask myself: what are all the things I perceive for which I have no concepts?

8

Or conversely: what are all the things I don't perceive because I have no concepts for them? After all, language took centuries to produce a concept like *red*–and in so doing it did not describe a sensation but a thing. Something is like something. As red as blood, white as milk, black as coal. And so forth.

9

Perception and apperception: passive perception and reflective perception, according to Leibniz–with reflective perception representing its higher version. It's perfectly possible for me to live in a red world without perceiving red. Or to become consciously absorbed in the red of a rose and to make it part of my world. I let it exert its influence on me. I feel it. I respond on the same wavelength. I am affected by it.

10

I am affected by a sensation. In thinking I conceive. (*Affect* from Latin *afficere*, work upon; *conceive* from Latin *concipere*, take to oneself.) Language thinks for you, says Albrecht Fabri.

11

Art/science–thought/sensation: aren't these opposites which really are not at all? Linguistic relics from a past epoch? Obsolete like the dualisms space/time, cause/effect, quality/quantity, energy/matter, power/powerlessness?

12

All art should become science, and all science should become art: Schlegel's proposition also strikes me as suspect. The alternative to wrong antitheses cannot be no antitheses–or better, antonyms.

13

Benjamin Whorf dreamed of a new language which would usher in a new epoch: of a language of structured correlations. I can imagine this in terms of colors. Here there are, as in language, two different types of opposites. The first type is polar, the second complementary.

The polar opposition is that of white/black. Something is brightest, something is darkest. In language: yes/no. The complementary opposition is that of the complementary colors: yellow/blue, red/green. The colors not only contrast with each other but complement each other. In language, as I was saying: thought/sensation, conception/perception.

14

White and black are opposites per se. But they are linked by an (almost) inexhaustible number of nuances, of grays. Similarly, for each shade of yellow there is a corresponding shade of blue, and so forth. There is no color that cannot be transformed continuously into another.

All colors occur in series. In the case of black/white we speak of the open, in the case of hues, of the closed, series (of the color circle).

The two series together form the dimensions of the color solid: white and black at the north and south poles, the color circle at the equator. On and in this solid all points (that is, all conceivable nuances) are precisely determinable: a closed system of structured correlations (thank you, Philipp Otto Runge!).

What the new language would have to do is this: create, like the color solid, a system of continuous concepts which is complete in itself.

15

It is no wonder that for Goethe colors were the model of a spiritual world which is perceived through concrete vision or, as we said, is directly perceptible information. More than a hundred years were to pass before art drew the logical conclusions. Max Bill is one of the pioneers whose importance will astonish people yet.

(For Max Bill's seventieth birthday, published in the Südwest-Presse, *Ulm, 22 December 1978)*

The Precision of Sensation

Heinrich von Kleist *(Über das Marionettentheater)*: "I said that, however skilled he might be with his paradoxes, he would never again make me believe that more gracefulness could be contained in a mechanical doll than in the structure of the human body. He retorted that it would simply be impossible for man even to equal the doll in this. Only a god could measure himself with matter in this field."

* * *

Man has eaten of the fruit of the Tree of Knowledge–lost the innocence of his ignorance without gaining the omniscience of God. Even so, sin allows him, if not to attain knowledge of the absolute, at least to attain absolute knowledge.

Pythagoras's theorem is an absolute piece of knowledge, like every mathematical formula.

* * *

Every formula is an indefinable fraction of the insight into creation. It may be pregnant with consequences or have none at all: that is a question of its originality. Whatever else, it is logically consistent: that is its definition.

A formula which is not right
is not a formula
which is not right, but not a formula
at all.

* * *

A formula is a truth *sui generis*. That is why mathematics occupies a special position among all sciences. It is true that even here every new insight takes the place of an old one. But the old one does not for that reason forfeit its content of truth, its correctness; at the most it loses its contemporary significance.

Is it any different in art?

It is true that every new form of painting replaces an old one–but the old one does not for that reason lose its content of truth, its validity.

* * *

Sometimes this process of replacement is spectacular–and not only in the most recent history. For example, when Raphael overshadowed his master Perugino. But this did not result in Perugino's pictures being driven out of currency. On the contrary: compared with the cult of Raphael early in the last century, nobody talks much of his art nowadays, whereas Perugino's has gained in topicality–which will certainly change again with time.

What is newly created in art does not take the place of the old but is added to it.

* * *

34

A mathematics
which is not an art
is not a mathematics either.

Mathematics is a double art: *ars inveniendi* and *ars demonstrandi*. First discover problems and then solve them. That the one is not synonymous with the other is shown by the history of the four-color problem. It was discovered a good hundred years ago, but we have only been able to solve it today (with the aid of the computer).

Art (as I understand it) is a double mathematics: first discover pictures and second–well, they don't have to be proved, but they must be realized so that they work out without leaving a remainder; like a mathematical formula.

* * *

According to Konrad Farner, art and science are opposites. But they have a basic criterion in common: "to be an exemplary draft of reality." In terms of science this implies: model as analogy, something like something; in terms of art, model as symbol, something for something. Art and science are in dialectical polarity, because both are "two sides, two possibilities of a deepened knowledge of world reality."

* * *

"All art should become science and all science become art," said Friedrich Schlegel in the "Athenäums-Fragmenten."

Certainly, the postulate is tied to a specific age and springs from the thinking of an idealistic general peacemaker. All-round caution should be exercised: Whatever has been said about art at any time has always been put out of currency by art itself. "Art need not do anything and may do everything," said the materialistic dissector Ernst Fischer (with the reservation that even this proposition might in turn be called in question).

* * *

If I speak of mathematics as my favorite science, I must add that I understand nothing of it. And every attempt to alter this has led me to realize that I am hopelessly untalented. What I understand is what Andreas Speiser called "the mathematical way of thinking." That is to say: to apply logical thought to life outside mathematics; to reflect on problems until they are completely intelligible–as I said: until they work out without a remainder.

Art and mathematics are complementarily different; that is to say: they differ from each other just as much as they complement each other. Mathematics is the discipline par excellence in the realm of the abstract of thought; art is the discipline par excellence in the realm of the sensuous sensation.

* * *

The elements of mathematics (numbers and signs) are axiomatic: those of the artist (colors and forms) are phenomenal–the one as absolutely determinable as the other.

As far as the instruments are concerned there is nothing to prevent the artist from designing pictures which are as precise as formulae. Whether it is right and wise to make use of them is another question. For my part, I cannot see why sensation should be less precise than thought.

And if it is the intention to evoke precise sensations by means of pictures, it can be done only if the pictures themselves are precise.

* * *

If a picture works out without a remainder, that means that all its elements are logically related to each other; it means that each color corresponds to every other, each form to every other, each form to every color and both color and form to their contents.

It means ultimately: that its structure is homogeneous, from conception to perception.

My dream: to make pictures which are completely constructed in every respect–without the construction being perceptible. In other words: I want to refine the construction to the point where–so to speak–it alters its state, quantities change into qualities; in fine: to surmount construction with construction.

To construct comes from *construere* = to pile up in layers. Example: in the Color Sounds the colors do not lie side by side as is usual but are arranged in layers one on top of the other. And the gradations are so small that the individual nuances melt into one another. They begin to oscillate, to fluoresce–and, precisely in this way, to acquire a new quality.

* * *

Is an art art "before it constructs its works completely?" (See page 27.)

Like thought, sensation is also a cultural achievement which is in a constant process of development. Anyone pondering over the matter will do well to consider origins. And whoever looks for origins will return willy-nilly to the ancient world where knowledge about the cause and effect of art–along with so much else–was highly developed.

Art which does not produce effects does not exist even as *l'art pour l'art*.

* * *

Aristotle demanded from the theater not distraction but composure. From tragedy he expected a cathartic effect: that through fear and pity there would be a purgation of precisely these and similar emotions.

The music of the ancient Greeks was conditioned from the outset, in three styles: one which inspired to heroic deeds, one which produced equanimity, and one which dissolved the listener into ecstasy–so much so, indeed, that the soul left the body and became united with the divine.

Music impassions or soothes, dissolves the listener into ecstasy...

* * *

Guiseppe Zarolini (in *Institutioni armonichi*; Venice, 1558): "The wise ones of the ancient world... called the Dorian mode stable, grave, and strict, and applied it to subjects which are serious and full of wisdom. For joyful and light-hearted things they used the Phrygian mode, in which there are smaller modulations than in all the other modes and a more definite point of view. These two styles were lauded and recognized by Plato and Aristotle, who held the other modes to be superfluous."

Even so, it is interesting to look at the other modes–and the effects they were credited with–because all together they form a logically coherent system.

36

The Dorian mode (e′ to e) is the expression of virility, strength of character, and courage.

The Phrygian (d′ to d) is cheerful, stirring,
the Lydian (c′ to c) is graceful,
the Mixolydian (b′ to b) is plangent,
the Hypodoric (a′ to a) is chivalrous,
the Hypophrygian (g′ to g) is soft and erotic,
the Hypolydian (f′ to f) is bacchantic.

Egon Friedell (in *Kulturgeschichte Griechenlands*): "The susceptibility and sensitivity of the Greeks to the power of musical tones must, by our standards, have been little less than pathological."

The Greeks even played music for mating horses: the so-called "horse-mating melody"; they thought that in this way more beautiful foals would be produced.

... helps to produce more beautiful foals...

Reports of cures through musical treatment are too numerous and too serious for them to have been simply poetical legends.

* * *

Friedell's supposition has today become certainty: therapy through music is a branch of research which is highly topical.

... and heals.

From a report in *Die Welt* (6 July 1979): "The man was an old officer; a stroke had left him with both legs paralyzed. In a Hamburg hospital physiotherapists tried to cure his inability to walk; but no reflexes in the legs were visible either on the wall-bars or in response to drumming. Moreover, the man was so depressed that he was less than half-hearted in his efforts.

"Then–more to cheer the patient up than as part of a method–they played him a tape of an evergreen: 'O Donna Clara,' his favorite tune. The result was astounding: he grew radiant, moved his legs to the rhythm and a little later was running about the room–It's just like Lourdes, said a nurse."

The President of the Hamburg Academy of Music, Professor Hermann Raue, is convinced after extensive research that "Music can do a great deal to cure the lame." Raue found that the pieces of music producing favorable results were those that the patient had liked in his adolescence–irrespective of whether they were pops or classics.

* * *

The magical power of these pieces to bring about a cure does not consist in their artistic value but rather in an indefinable emotional affinity.

I am reminded of the Black Madonna of Rocamadour, who has worked innumerable miracles; but as a work of art she is unprepossessing.

* * *

A distinction must be made between the sensitivity of the soul and the sensitivity of the senses.

The sensation of the senses is sensuous and mediated by the eye, the ear, the nose, the mouth, the skin. The sensation of the soul is love, jealousy, anger, pain, shame–the world of feelings.

* * *

Using conceptual associations, the psychologist Rudolf Hofstätter has tried to find out which sensations of the senses and the soul correspond to each other. One result of his investigations: the polarity profiles of the color red and the concept "love" are almost identical–in which context it is interesting to note that the saying, "Love is red," is scientifically confirmed.

Stimulus and sensation in the realm of the senses and in the realm of the soul

38

The sensations of the soul are something immediate; they "come over me." I am "smitten" by love–whether I will or not: "I blush scarlet." I "am petrified" with fear–and become pale. I am "overcome" by pain, "seized" by desire, "quiver" with rage. I am "stricken" with grief and am "filled" with happiness. Language does not leave me an opportunity to reflect consciously on the sensations of the soul; I can acquire detachment (at best) only in retrospect.

* * *

It is no mere accident that language makes no sharp distinction between the sensation of the stimulus and the sensation of the feeling; if one thinks of the "totality of the combined psychological actions of phenomena" (Eckhart Heimendahl).

According to Kandinsky the soul is the piano and the eye the hammer which causes the strings to sound

Kandinsky designates feelings like joy, sorrow, and so forth as material states of the soul. "The tones of colors, like those of music, are of a much finer nature and arouse much finer vibrations of the soul, which cannot be described in words."

* * *

Heimendahl: "We do not really see every color our eye sees. It is only when we look at it, or if it forces itself upon our attention, that we see color properly, that is to say: we become conscious of it on noticing it. In conscious perception readiness and the *intention*–experience directed to the color–are crucial cofactors."

* * *

The sensitization of the senses bears witness to a high level of consciousness, and hence, of culture. That is the realm of art; by which is meant not only music and the visual arts but also the art of taste, the art of cooking, for instance; the art of smell (curious that this realm of the senses has never been properly defined, never become a discipline); and the tactile art (the art of love).

* * *

Every moment a hundred thousand impressions impinge upon me. And every moment I make a selection from among these impressions; the fraction of a fraction of them penetrates my conscious mind. I perceive a stimulus. The stimulus becomes sensation.

Leibniz distinguishes between perception and apperception: between "mere" and "conscious" sensation. I believe another distinction is necessary: "exact" sensation.

Unconscious sensation and conscious sensation

By conscious sensation I understand: to register a stimulus. I do not hear a note as "merely" more or less low or high but as C, C sharp, D, and so forth. I do not hear it as merely loud or soft, light or dark, but I consciously register: how loud, how light.

* * *

Another example: of two different shades of gray, one is necessarily light, one darker, and there is one somewhere in between. If I concentrate my attention on these colors I now have no difficulty in locating *where* between the other two the medium gray lies; nearer to the light or dark shade?–or in the middle?

By exact sensation I understand: to experience a stimulus. I not only register the note as C or C sharp, I am also aware of its effect. And the more carefully I listen, the more I feel its special character, and the more I therefore respond to it. Certainly, it is extremely difficult to articulate this effect. And no doubt the ideal case will remain the utopian one in which stimulus and sensation coincide.

Inexact sensation and exact sensation

Conscious sensation is, so to speak, metrical in nature, and exact sensation, psychological.

* * *

Malevich painted–in 1913–a black square in a white square. What he wanted to evoke in his beholder was not aesthetic pleasure in his composition, but the sensation of objectlessness.

The sensation of objectlessness...

For him the black square was the sensation, the white one the "void" outside this sensation.

For Malevich the sensations which come to life in man are stronger than man himself. At all costs they must break out; they must take shape. It is nothing but the sensation of speed–flight–which produced the aircraft: seeking a shape, a form.

This leitmotif attained its apotheosis in the later white square in a white square. For Malevich that was the *ultima ratio*, the greatest possible precision in giving expression to his idea of something so indeterminate.

* * *

No, the apotheosis came from Yves Klein, who in his monochromes did not even allow the hint of a form (apart from the boundary of the picture: the rectangle of the canvas is, of course, a form of the form).

By declaring an ultramarine blue, and nothing but an ultramarine blue, to be a picture, to be art, Klein challenges me as a beholder. I accept the challenge–and am surprised that my sensation penetrates ever more deeply. And no end is in sight.

I place Klein's blue in relation to myself, and vice versa: I place myself in relation to it. I feel its coolness, its depth, its detachment. I let it work upon me like temperature, I breathe it like air.

I feel that the personality of this blue has little to do with my own. I see myself rather as complementary to it, a warm red. But I am fascinated by the oppositeness of its originality, its intensity.

Of all the colors there are few that have so much character as ultramarine blue. It radiates calm. Balance. Timelessness. Spacelessness.

* * *

The Shah Mosque in Isfahan comes to my mind. The blue interior with the blue domes. Here, in the sphere in which I find myself–here form and color are one. No corners, no edges, no perspective; a room without dimensions, sensed rather than known; the blue sensation of inward communion, of composure.

Actually the sky should not be sky blue–it should be ultramarine blue.

I do not merely feel the coolness of this blue. I can also hear it; I can smell it; I can taste it.

The world does not exist outside me, but in me. As imagination of infinite extent. Yves Klein has shown me a door opening inward. In ultramarine blue, in red, in yellow–in every color is contained the universe of a sensation.

...and the objectlessness of sensation

40

In every stimulus, in fact. Blindly I pick one out of the multiplicity of appearances, perhaps strong, perhaps weak in character–that is immaterial. Perhaps it means something to me, perhaps it means nothing to me–that is material. For that depends on me.

What matters is this: how I look at the world. How I pass from the part to the whole, from chance to a system of structured connections. To a world view.

* * *

The right word occurred to Goethe at an early period: when he spoke about exact sensuous imagination.

In every stimulus is contained the universe of a sensation.

41

The Spirit of Colors: Goethe's *Theory of Colors*

(The Precision of Sensation, 2)

42

For over forty years Goethe worked on his *Theory of Colors*. The first publication appeared in 1971, the last in 1820. The principal work, consisting of three parts *(Zur Farbenlehre)* was published in 1810.

Newton's work *Opticks*, in which he showed that white light is a mixture of all the colors, appeared in 1704.

It was not easy for me to bring myself to study Goethe's *Theory of Colors*. I, too, shared the 150-year-old prejudice: that on this subject the Old Man was not to be regarded seriously; that he had taken an impossibly obdurate stand against Newton; that it was nothing but the obstinacy of old age that made him say to Eckermann: "I take no pride at all in what I have done as a poet. Excellent poets lived at the same time as myself; even finer poets lived before me, and others will follow me. But the fact that I am the only person in my own century who knows the truth in the difficult science of colors–that is something in which I take no little pride..."

True, the historical section of Goethe's *Theory of Colors* is easy, and can be read with profit and pleasure (and this is where anyone interested in the subject should start). But the didactic section–the heart of the work–is difficult to understand, if only because of its obsolete concepts. And the polemical part is now merely a literary curiosity, because of the zeal with which Goethe–he compares himself to Luther–sought to overcome the "obscurantism of the clerics" after "the error of Newton's theory" had been revealed to him.

Goethe's theory of colors is not a natural science. Andreas Speiser declared it to be a "liberal science belonging to art and analogous with the study of musical harmony."

* * *

Goethe's theory of colors is a strange science indeed. Ronald D. Gray has shown that the stock of ideas on which it is based is alchemical through and through (*Goethe the Alchemist*; Cambridge, 1962).

Faust bears truly eloquent testimony to the poet's familiarity with the rich imagery of this world. Mephisto introduces himself in these words: "Part of the part am I that once was whole, part of the darkness that gave birth to light."

The darkness "that once was whole" must be imagined as a condition prior to all else, as the "abyss and ground" of all being. As long as it reigned, it reigned over nothing but itself. Creation began only with the appearance of light (in the beginning was light, which was also Logos, the Word); in the field of tension created by the opposition of darkness and light.

Goethe calls this opposition polarity. In it he sees one of the great driving forces of all Nature. Colors arise neither from light alone nor from darkness. Rather, they are the product of the polarity between precisely these two opposites.

The colors are
the first schematisms of matter.
This proposition of Zeno
"is very welcome to us,"
wrote Goethe.

* * *

For light and darkness to bring forth colors, a medium is required, namely the "opaque" or "semi-opaque": a densification, as it were, of the light, or a rarefaction of the darkness.

In Goethe's world-picture light and darkness are universal entities, absolute and infinite. "Opaqueness" veils them and manifests them at the same time in colors.

The colors are individual units, relative and limited. Light is manifested in yellow and darkness in blue. These are the two "pure," original primary colors, from which all others are derived.

Opaqueness in all its degrees (a central concept of Goethe's theory of colors) is in principle operative everywhere as a medium. It is operative even where transparency might be thought to prevail, for instance, in the atmosphere through which we receive the light of the sun.

This example is in fact an everyday experience. We see how colors are not only generated but also modulated by opaqueness. On the horizon, where it is densest, it makes the sun appear red; as its density diminishes, it turns the red into yellow and then yellow into white.

Goethe:
"Place the most opaque
in the sunbeam's light,
And you see purple
as a pure delight."

When the sun reaches the zenith, when opaqueness is (relatively) most attenuated, there shines through for a time absolute whiteness–which we can feel but no longer see. And then from midday to evening we witness the whole spectacle again in reverse.

* * *

When opaqueness is in front of light, it produces the warm colors; when it is in front of darkness, it produces the cold.

Light is the sun, darkness is the black of interstellar space, which looks blue through the mediation of opaqueness. And it is a fact that the thinner this opaqueness–say, on a mountain peak–the deeper and redder the blue of the sky becomes until it finally turns into the black of outer space. (See André Bjerke, *Neue Beiträge zu Goethes Farbenlehre*; Stuttgart, 1961.)

* * *

Just as opaqueness works in air, so it also operates in glass, which as a prism generates colors. Not arbitrarily, however, but only when light and darkness meet.

When Goethe had to give back some prisms he had borrowed–the messenger was already at the door–he took a last look through them. "How surprised I was when I saw that the white wall seen through the prism still looked white and that only where it came up against something dark did a more or less definite color appear, and finally that the window bars appeared to be the most colorful of all."

That was the initial experience which led Goethe "instinctively" to the insight that the Newtonian theory was wrong. And which gave the impetus to his work on the theory of colors.

* * *

The breadth of the context in which Goethe envisaged the principle of polarity and the concept of opaqueness can be seen from a diary entry for 25 May 1817. Under the heading "Chromatic reflections and metaphors" he notes: "Love and hate, hope and fear are also nothing but different states of our opaque inner selves through which the spirit looks either on the light or the dark side. If we look through this opaque organic environment to the light, we love and we hope; if we look towards the dark, we hate and we fear."

All living things strive for color, for the particular, for specification, says Goethe. And Jakob Böhme (an early seventeenth century alchemist, whose work Goethe

Like air and glass, smoke, colorless in itself, is also an opaque medium. Goethe: "against a light background it appears yellow, before a dark one blue."

44

had read) wrote that every living thing is a limited phenomenon which endeavors to be something.

Color stands for beginning, for energy and day. Conversely the fading of color means finality, death, night. Riemer and Humboldt recorded a conversation with Goethe on the subject of death:

Light, which creates color out of darkness, is an excellent symbol of the soul, which animates matter and out of it creates the body. As the fading of the red glow from the evening cloud which leaves a gray rack behind, so is the death of man. The light of the soul grows dim and diffuses out of the fabric of the body.

* * *

Sometimes Goethe refers to colors as the "actions and sufferings of light": the polarity of active and passive which arises from the original polarity of expanding light and contracting darkness. If it were not for this duality, there could be neither spatial determination, no "here" and "there," nor temporal discrimination, no "before" and "after."

Light as one pole is positive, active, warm; darkness as the other is negative, passive, cold. What is contained in black and white characterizes blue and yellow, which are derived from them directly, in a heightened form. Goethe marks the contrast with the poles + and −, and develops this idea (quite in the tradition of the alchemists):

plus	minus
yellow	blue
effectiveness	deprivation
light	shadow
bright	dark
power	weakness
warmth	cold
proximity	distance
repulsion	attraction
related to acids	related to alkalis

Blue and yellow are the original colors. According to Goethe, there is then a heightening through which both approach a third; by this process there emerges on either side a deepest and a highest, a simplest and a most complex, a basest and a noblest.

In terms of actual colors the deepest, simplest, and basest is green; the highest, most complex, and noblest is red.

See also Metachrome 3.22, In memory of Goethe, page 129.

45

Goethe:
"I have no objection to anyone's thinking he can feel color...
It can also be tasted.
Blue will taste alkaline, yellow-red acid.
There is an affinity among all manifestations of being."

Green originates–according to Goethe–from mixing blue and yellow. In green the characteristics of blue and yellow do not cancel each other out, "but are brought to the point of equilibrium where neither can be discriminated and consequently the mixture acquires a specific quality for the eye; it appears as a union which no longer recalls the composition. This union we call green."

Red is different, being produced by the condensation–heightening–of blue and yellow.

See also Purple Balance, In memory of Goethe, page 105

The process may be visualized as follows: blue and yellow–arising from black and white through the veil of opaqueness–produce in turn through the veil of opaqueness a new stage of heightening, first yellow-red and blue-red, which, after passing through further stages, unite to form red. In red the characteristics of blue and yellow are entirely absorbed and become heightened to form a new individuality.

In green the eye, the senses, experience real satisfaction; in red the union of the heightened poles, not only the senses but also the spirit, finds ideal satisfaction and fulfilment.

Heightening, says Goethe, is the second great driving force of Nature. Accordingly green is the culmination in the basest; red in the noblest. A general law is manifested in red: namely, that the original duality can be transformed by the process of heightening into a new individuality, a new union.

* * *

Red–Goethe often calls it purple, or, more precisely: "the carmine that dries on a white dish of porcelain"–is for him "the highest of all color phenomena." In it are contained all other colors, "partly *actu*, partly *potentia*." "Its effect is as unique as its nature. It gives an impression both of gravity and dignity and of grace and charm; the former it creates in its dark, condensed state and the latter in its light, attenuated state. And thus the dignity of age and the charm of youth can be invested in One Color."

* * *

Jakob Weder takes the comparison a step further with the signs of magnetic fields of force and, on the analogy of blue − and yellow +, he attaches − + to green and + − to red.

* * *

The *Theory of Colors*, says Goethe, is not only to be read but also put into practice. And he straightway gives an example: in his house at Weimar he had the various rooms painted in different colors. Guests he did not like were never admitted beyond the cold-blue "Juno room," so that they would soon depart. Blue evokes not only a sense of cold but also of emptiness, of distance. It seems to recede from the beholder whereas a warm color like yellow comes forward to meet him.

Those who were invited to a meal were taken beyond the first room into the festive dining room, which was warm yellow. Yellow inspires not only a sense of warmth but also of fullness and proximity. And above all of cheerfulness: there always seems to be a little sunshine in a yellow room.

Goethe used to work in the green garden room. He felt that green was neutral; this color did not distract him. It is a source of quiet visual contentment. The eye is soothed by it, "one does not desire, nor is one able, to go any farther." Under its influence the spirit grows at peace with things as they are, with reality, and it does not seek beyond for a spiritual meaning (Gray, *Goethe the Alchemist*).

* * *

Just as color works from the inside outward, revealing the inner state through outward appearance, so it also works from the outside inward. According to Goethe, colors affect the human mind and, depending on their character, induce in it moods which are "sometimes lively and aspiring, sometimes soft and yearning, sometimes uplifted to the noble, sometimes dragged down to the base"–the effect of yellow, blue, red and green.

Not only his *Theory of Colors*, but the whole corpus of his literary work bears witness to Goethe's understanding of colors.

If a boy is dressed half in black and half in pink (as in *Was wir bringen*), this is no coincidence but a symbol: the dark side stands for tragedy, the light for comedy; black for death, pink for young life, the first stage on the path to mature, passionate red. (See Peter Schmidt, *Goethes Farbensymbolik*; Berlin, 1965.)

* * *

On the one hand Goethe distinguishes among the sensuous, moral, and aesthetic effect; on the other among the allegorical, symbolic, and mystic use of color.

He calls red a symbol of majesty, green an allegory of hope. The symbol is an image coinciding with reality; the allegory stands for reality only by a convention which one must know in order to understand its meaning. The

Goethe quotes a "witty Frenchman," whose conversational tone with Madame has not been the same since she changed the furniture of her room, which was blue, into crimson.

symbol is an open, the allegory a cryptic, secret. It would be wrong to see Goethe's color symbolism as a rigid system in which each color is assigned a clearly defined meaning. Goethe was aware of the ambivalence inherent in the curious fact that every color has a broad spectrum of meanings which, not infrequently, are contradictory.

Red indicates love just as much as hate; blue fidelity as well as infidelity; yellow stands for cheerfulness as well as envy; green stands for both hope and for poison; the bridal dress is white as is the shroud.

In conclusion: "We have an inkling that, in the end, color is also open to a mystical interpretation." We have an inkling of what Goethe means by this. But he does not go more deeply into the matter, so as not to incur "the suspicion of extravagant speculation."

* * *

As far as I am concerned, the key to an understanding of *Theory of Colors* is not–*pace* Goethe–to see it as a contribution to scientific research, whatever the branch, but rather as a mythology of Goethe's most intimate and personal kind. Its content is not derived from objective facts which are right or wrong. Its truth is indwelling. Its basic idea is rigorous and clear, its components are of inexhaustible variety. It is an epic: it must be read like *Faust*.

Unlike the tragedy of human inadequacy, the *Theory of Colors* is a model and a symbol of genesis, insight into the perfection of divine creation. In our experience of colors and in our knowledge of the laws underlying them we penetrate to the ultimates that hold all life together–from the origin, evolution, and structure of the cosmos to the moral category in which individual colors produce their ethical/aesthetic effect.

48

Goethe:
"Light and spirit, the one dominant
in the physical
and the other in the moral,
are the highest indivisible energies."

Color
and the Colors

(The Precision of Sensation, 3)

In his *Theory of Harmony* (1911) Arnold Schönberg interprets the history of music as the development of harmony–via octaves, fifths, thirds–into ever-higher regions of the overtones.

Schönberg: The most perfect concord (after unison) is the tone that comes earliest in the harmonic series, therefore occurs most frequently, and thus sounds the loudest: the octave. The next most perfect is the fifth, then the major third.

In this connection the concepts of consonance and dissonance must be regarded with reserve. The antithesis they denote is false; the difference is not one of principle but of gradation. Schönberg: The essential thing is the analytic ability of the ear to familiarize itself with the more remote harmonics.

How true: Schönberg himself has become a classic; today his music sounds as familiar to us as Beethoven's– who in his time was a musical revolutionary; say, in a symphony (his first) which he began with a diminished seventh.

Harmony is a process of familiarization

* * *

On the one hand it is astonishing how slowly the development proceeded (or should one say: how difficult the process of familiarization is?). In the thirteenth century they reached the third. In the sixteenth century chromaticism (from *chroma*, color) appeared, the richer, "colored" palette. In the prelude to Wagner's *Tristan* even the common chord of the principal key no longer figures because everything is dissolved in chromaticism. In the course of the nineteenth century the ground tone or fundamental was dethroned; in Schönberg's twelve-tone music it disappears. From there a direct line leads to the sound synthesizer, which produces several hundred tones per octave–indeed, as many as the ear can distinguish: as far as the available material is concerned, this is the "end of the road."

It is astonishing, on the other hand, how quickly things have begun to move since everything became possible. Schönberg anticipated the future by fifty or sixty years with his prophecy, "the concept of euphony as material for art is so expanded that the whole natural phenomenon (of tones) has a place within it."

* * *

Music has always been more strictly codified than the visual arts. Parallels in development do not immediately leap to mind but they do exist. In musical tones as in color there was the steadily greater penetration into the subject matter, the steadily increasing mastery in handling all possible nuances. In the case of color–to stay with this example–an "end of the road" of a kind is coming into view: calculability and electronic generation on a display screen of all the hues the eye can distinguish.

Previous stages: Giotto, Leonardo, Titian.

Giotto
releases color
from its symbolic content

Giotto released color from its Byzantine rigidity, from its function as a symbolic medium. He made it a characteristic of Nature, man and object, body and space.

Leonardo brought insight into chiaroscuro, the light-and-dark of color.

Titian
discovers color as color

Titian used color not as a medium for representing Nature; he felt that color itself was something naturelike. Theodor Hetzer: By following his genius, Titian set to work like Nature itself; that is to say, he organized color as a metaphor of natural structure.

Monet
recognizes color
as the expression of light

Titian stood at the beginning of an epoch, at whose end a few names are collected in my entirely personal imaginary museum: Runge, Turner, Seurat, Van Gogh, Cézanne, Monet; Monet above all: the haystacks, Rouen cathedral, the water lilies–first and foremost the room in the Museum of Modern Art.

* * *

Like Schönberg in music, Kandinsky marks the start of a new epoch in visual art. The one freed composition from the ground tone; the other liberated painting from its objects. Kandinsky reduced pictures to the means of representation. He declared the foreground (the immediately apparent) to be what it had always been: the background (the true inwardness), or in his words, the spiritual in art–to which a dictum of Albrecht Fabri might be added: The formal (I include color) which has not already been content simply does not exist.

Kandinsky
liberates color from objects

* * *

Mondrian reduced the means of representation to the irreducible: to line and plane, to vertical/horizontal, to black/white, to red/yellow/blue. He created for himself a vocabulary of "pure" elements because he regarded this as the basis for creating "pure harmonies." The equilibrium of the duality, the individual and the universe.

Mondrian
reduces color to the most elemental

His elements are elemental only by personal interpretation. The lines are not geometrical lines but often variants of the bar; and what he called the primary colors must remain controversial to this day–quite apart from the fact that his yellows, blues and reds were shaded in a highly personal way. But it will be acknowledged that his choices are neutral and objective.

* * *

The curious thing is this: Mondrian created this vocabulary–and used it in the most subjective manner conceivable.

He designed his "compositions" without any recognizable syntax. His friends are unanimous in their testimony that he worked on each one of them for months. That is to say, he shifted the elements millimeters and fractions of millimeters–until the harmony was declared perfect in the court of his feeling.

In distinction, not to say in opposition, to Vantongerloo. The difference between them is categorical, even though, in the De Stijl period of the twenties, their works looked similar. Confusingly so in the eyes of many.

Vantongerloo not only used geometric elements like Mondrian. He also joined them geometrically. That is to say, each of his pictures–and his sculptures–is based on a kind of formula, a basic constructive idea. Even when Vantongerloo's pictures later ceased to have any look of "elemental geometry" about them–unlike Mondrian's –they remained at heart, in their basic thought, much more constructive than Mondrian's pictures ever were.

The profound difference between Mondrian and Vantongerloo is also visible on the surface: Mondrian's pictures became pastose on being worked over; Vantongerloo's paintings are smooth with no recognizable corrections.

* * *

Mondrian and Vantongerloo are representatives of a formal art, just as all constructive art, up to the fifties, was determined by form, or rather, by formal structures.

Representatives of a colored art are Albers and Rothko. The difference between them is similar to that between Mondrian and Vantongerloo–except that it is obvious.

It surprises no one to see the "constructor" in Albers. Albers paints his colors evenly in squares, Rothko in patches in a "painterly" manner.

* * *

But–something which is less obvious–Albers is not a constructor because of the square. The whole point and uniqueness of his art stems rather from the fact that he has brought a constructive element into color.

Each of his pictures is a discovery in the largely unexplored nature of colors. Each represents a phenomenon recognized as *clare et distincte*. The crucial element in Albers's *Homage to the Square* pictures is not the three or four colors of which they consist materially, but the specific and diverse ways in which they are correlated: the "interaction of color," which he explored with ultimate precision and made subservient to his ends.

Albers opened up a new dimension. Like no one before him, he examined the phenomenon of color with competence and commitment.

* * *

That this should not have happened until our century is surprising and at the same time an example of the way in which, with advancing knowledge, the object of knowledge becomes steadily more elemental. To this extent there is indeed a somewhat closer parallel to the development of music. It is not breadth that is sought but depth.

* * *

If it is color rather than colors on which my sights are set, I have to look further back, as far as I can: into the dim and distant past when there were literally no colors.

* * *

52

Albers
explores color as phenomenon

From history
back into prehistory

In the beginning a color could not be designated by a concept of its own; it was like something: red as blood, white as snow, black as ebony.

Obviously, in snowless regions other references had to be found. In the land of the Bible the idea of white as the color of milk became established–which is not surprising among a people of herdsmen and farmers (Roland Gradwohl, *Colors in the Old Testament*).

* * *

Gradwohl: It is remarkable that in spite of all the wealth of names for different colors, the Old Testament has no special term for the concept of color. The reason for the absence of an abstract concept is that the individual colors were still not conceived as abstract entities but rather as components, as the outer coverings of objects. In many Indo-European languages the word for color is identical with the word for covering, skin.

Color as covering, skin

* * *

According to the method of analogy, language is as rich in nuances as the models Nature supplies.

Color as analogy

Lemon yellow differs from canary yellow just as the yellow of the lemon differs from that of the canary: a difference that is barely perceptible. But within this nuance there are still sulfur, vanilla, saffron, sunflower and quince yellow.

In the following nuance–toward red–the yellows are called marsh marigold, butter, straw, maize, egg, topaz, brass, golden, and apricot yellow.

* * *

Analogies such as these have always produced others, mainly on the principle of the preeminent case. Example: yellow-gold-sun. The planet is the brightest of the planets, just as the metal is the brightest of the metals, and as the color is the brightest of the colors.

The seven steps to the sanctuary of the temple of Sargon at Khorsabad (Mesopotamia, c. 800 B.C.) were painted in colors corresponding to the seven metals, which corresponded to the seven planets:

yellow	gold	Sol
white	silver	Luna
red	iron	Mars
mixed	quicksilver	Mercury
blue	tin	Jove
green	copper	Venus
black	lead	Saturn

53

After color had been *like* something, an analogy, it came to stand *for* something. It became a symbol.

Jove–Thursday *(jeudi, giovedì)*
tin–blue–shadow–among the alchemists stands for "marking/thinking."

Mars–Tuesday (*mardi, martedì*)
iron–red–fire–stands for "seeking/desiring."

Venus–Friday (*vendredi, venerdì*)
copper–hiding of the light–stands for "hoping/expecting."

Sol–Sunday
gold–lights–stands for "finding/recognizing."

Luna–Monday *(lundi, lunedi)*
silver–white–clarity–stands for "possessing/enjoying."

Saturn–Saturday
lead–black–darkness–stands for "forgetting/renouncing."

Mercury–Wednesday (*mercredi, mercoledì*)
quicksilver–occupies a special position: quicksilver is held to be the seed of all metals.

(From Naturae naturantis et naturatae Mysterium, *author unknown; Berlenberg, 1725. Quoted from: Ronald D. Gray*, Goethe the Alchemist *with additions.)*

* * *

For Aristotle there were three "simple" colors: white, yellow, and black, "which accompany the elements, fire, air, water, and earth. Air and water are by nature white, fire and the sun yellow, earth black."

According to Leonardo there are six simple colors:

white and black	= light and darkness
yellow	= earth
green	= water
blue	= air
red	= fire.

* * *

According to Johann Zahn's book on color symbolism (late seventeenth century),

white	= fire, God
yellow	= ether, angel
red	= air, man
blue	= water, animal
black	= earth, plant.

* * *

One of the oldest correlations is that of the ancient typology of temperaments and colors:

choleric:	yellow-red
melancholic:	red-blue
phlegmatic:	blue-green
sanguine:	green-yellow.

* * *

In Goethe's color tetrahedron (1816) we find
green for sensuousness
yellow for reason
blue for understanding
red for imagination.

* * *

Given Goethe's world of imagery, it is almost automatic–provided one knows something about it and is initiated into it–to equate red with imagination. Red (more precisely: the carmine dried in the white porcelain dish) contains for the poet–partly *actu*, partly *potentia*–all other colors. For Goethe it is the zenith of the heightening process (in Russian *red* is synonymous with *beautiful*), just as imagination is among human faculties.

* * *

Other authors have a different arrangement. C.G. Jung, for example, correlates colors with his archetypes:

blue:	thinking
red:	feeling
yellow:	intuition
green:	sensation.

The correspondences for blue and green are closely parallel to Goethe's; in the case of those for yellow and red room must be left for interpretation.

* * *

"That a language is really only symbolic, only pictorial and never expresses objects directly but only by reflection" holds true both for colors and language and also for the language of colors, for the elucidation of which Goethe put this sentence to paper.

Color as language

However, in this reflection there is a great deal to be perceived, as when, for instance, language formulates: love is red, blood is red, the devil is red in his rage.

Love and rage have one thing in common: they drive the blood to the head; they make one go red–in which context the connection between red and blood can be traced back to the beginning. Gradwohl: Among the terms for red the root '*dm* is found most often. It is not possible to prove a grammatical connection between *'dm* and *dàm*, 'blood', but it probably exists.

Red

Red is excitement, alarm, struggle, conquest, fanaticism; in each case, activity. And warmth, presence.

* * *

Blue

Blue is fidelity, language goes on to formulate. This may be because blue originates in the depths: the deeper the sky and water–in themselves colorless– the bluer and darker they seem to be; constant and motionless.

Blue is also infidelity: to go off into the blue. This may be because things grow blue with distance. The farther off the intrinsically green hills of the landscape, the bluer and lighter they appear to be; hazy and melting into vapor. And smoke–colorless in itself–also looks blue when it rises against a dark background.

Blue is longing, purity, absorption, fatalism; in each case, passivity. And coolness, timelessness.

("Blue Monday," a German expression meaning a Monday off work, has a factual origin: the indigo dyers dyed their fabrics on Friday, and because indigo dying is an oxidative process, it takes time–namely, Saturday, Sunday, and Monday–for the fabrics to become blue. Monday was free.)

* * *

Even if the reflection of other colors in language is less evident, it is still recognizable.

Yellow and green

The German says yellow with envy, whereas the Englishman says green with envy. Both may be connected with the bile which rises and makes one look yellow-green.

Or, green is hope.

After the white death-sleep of winter, Nature is filled with life again; it becomes green. Green–related to "grow"–means in its original sense what is fresh and growing in Nature and therefore the opposite of what is dry and faded and of what is already fully grown and mature. Immaturity is therefore the reverse side of green: the greenhorn.

* * *

I know violet comes from *viola–violetta*–the flower violet. But it cannot be denied that the association with violate and violence on the one hand and with violin and viola on the other lies in the character of this color.

Purple is derived from porphyra, the purple snail. Yet pure also means unadulterated, unalloyed–and in this connection we must recall the charisma of this color in Roman/Byzantine times.

* * *

To follow the traces color has left in language is one way of learning something of its secret. Another is to determine the sensations it elicits by means of experiments.

Since psychology embarked on this path, since the time of Wilhelm Wundt, a hundred years ago or so, it has had difficulties in obtaining results. However, the contrast between exciting and soothing inherent in the colors red and blue is beyond question.

Stefanescu-Goanga (a pupil of Wundt): In the case of red, orange, yellow, and purple, excitement must be regarded as the constant and main affective value, whereas with green, blue, indigo, and violet the power to soothe is uppermost. And excitement occurs in its purest form in red, while among the soothing feelings the purest form is to be sought in blue.

* * *

Supporting experiments have shown that the pulse is faster when red is contemplated and slower when blue is contemplated.

Under the influence of red, time is overestimated' and weights seem heavier. Under the influence of blue time is underestimated, and weights seem lighter.

Red represents a stimulus to mental activity. It mediates an excellent atmosphere for creating ideas; blue is more suitable for putting ideas into action.

The energy of red has a marked influence on the growth of plants. It accelerates the development of certain of the lower animals, enhances hormonal and sexual activity, and heals wounds *(Faber Birren,* Color Psychology and Therapy; *New York, 1950)*.

Color as a medium of biology

* * *

At the turn of the century the Danish physician Niels Ryberg Finsen investigated the effect of light on the living organism; he started "photo- or chromotherapy," and tried to cure diseases like tuberculosis of the skin and smallpox with light of specific wavelengths. Finsen received an early Nobel prize for his work. What developed from these beginnings I have been unable to ascertain.

Color as a medium of physiology

* * *

I heard from Gaston Déribéré, of Paris, a technician, designer, and promoter of an astonishing experiment: he tried to find out whether the blind could tell if their immediate environment changed color.

To this end he constructed rooms with walls consisting of vertical bars. These bars were triangular in section–one side yellow, one red, one blue–and could be rotated 120 degrees at a time; in this way the color temperature of the room could be changed in a fraction of a second.

Déribéré assured me that the blind were invariably right in stating which color was showing, which suggests that the effect of color is mediated not only by a sensory impression but also via radiation, by vibration on the wavelength specific to the color.

     * * *

According to the color psychologist Max Lüscher, red stands for drive, action; blue for contentment, sensitivity of feeling.

To prefer red in the Lüscher Test indicates activity; to reject red, overstimulation in the psychic working-over of experience, fear of being beset by insoluble problems.

To prefer blue in the Lüscher Test indicates need of rest; to reject blue, disquiet, the wish to avoid ties of affection.

As a counterpart to red/blue, green/yellow forms the second pair of complementary colors. Green stands for tension, yellow for release.

     * * *

If we correlate the sensations evoked by colors with the closed color circle we shall hardly be surprised to find that these reactions in turn form something like a closed system.

Violet: tension disquiet	

Red: excitement
     drive
	Blue: calm
	      perseverance

Orange: exuberance
      pleasure
	Blue-green: devotion
	      mourning

Yellow: liberation
     joy
	Green: equanimity
	      repose

	Green-yellow: composure content

Certainly, there is something significant about these correspondences between colors and emotions (where pure colors are concerned), but the system they represent is nowhere near complete.

Even very minor deviations can alter the psychological effect of a color quite fundamentally. A pure yellow mixed with a trace of black gives a color between mustard yellow and olive, both of them shades which have hardly anything in common with the original color; indeed, the freshness and radiance of yellow is converted into its opposite, into the dull and moldy.

Anyone seeking a systematic arrangement in these questions will generally find that the addition of darkness to light colors will alter their character disproportionately, as will an addition of light to dark colors.

Blue–the color of mystic absorption–lightened to sky blue forms the "charming nothing," as Goethe called it. A dark red-violet is elegiac; Wundt ascribes to it a touch of gloomy, melancholy seriousness. This alters radically if the violet is lightened: the color becomes shrill, intrusive, vulgar.

Red, midway between light and dark, reacts the most sensitively to all kinds of changes. Mixed with a trace of black, it yields red-brown, which means calm after excitement. Lightened to salmon-pink, it means–according to Lüscher–readiness, openness to stimulation. Red also reacts sensitively to a small change of color temperature. Toward warm/orange: stimulation becomes agitation, passion gives way to feverishness; toward cold/magenta: stimulation is pent up, energy is held back, passion gives way to restraint.

Green, like red midway between light and dark, reacts–to my mind–least sensitively, and thereby confirms its character of equanimity, of repose.

Pure colors evoke elementary sensations. But it is the intermediate shades that count

The colors not only evoke sensations. They are themselves sensitive

59

Pictures

Karl Gerstner's work–for all its apparent homogeneity–consists in the development of ideas, pictorial ideas, which clearly differ from one another. At the instigation of André Kamber, he described them in the catalog to his first retrospective (Museum of Fine Arts, Solothurn, 1978), dividing them into nine chapters:

1. The Aperspectives
2. The Serial Pictures
3. The Carro Pictures
4. The Metachromes
5. The Apparatuses
6. The AlgoRhythms
7. The Color Sounds
8. The Color Forms
9. The Color Lines

The following introductions to the individual chapters are taken from the Solothurn catalog and updated where necessary. By way of introduction to the introductions Karl Gerstner wrote:

"It is relatively simple to date the beginning of each chapter. And difficult (nay, impossible) to say where each ends. And for two reasons.

"The first: even today I am still carrying out projects which were conceived years ago. For instance, I allowed myself to be persuaded (it was a pleasure) by Hans Mayer to execute the cycle Finite-Infinite Series which was illustrated in its draft form in the catalog to the exhibition at Suzanne Bollag in 1961 [see pages 82 and 83].

"Why not?–the project has lost some of its topicality, no question about that. But I have always given quality priority over topicality as a criterion–which allows me to fill in the gaps in my work with an easy mind.

"The second reason: it has always been good fun for me to pursue an idea for as long as it is still capable of development, as long as I can wring a new aspect out of it. If I begin a new chapter, that is no reason, I feel, for closing any previous one. Sometimes it happens that I recommence the pursuit of a line which I thought I had given up long before without feeling that I must account to myself for what I am doing."

So much for the quotation. The introductions to the individual chapters are supplemented by other texts which have been written as occasion required; all the texts together form a virtually complete collection of Karl Gerstner's statements on his pictures. "The Color-Form Continuum" (in chapter 8) was written for this book.

H. St.

Dimensions are given in millimeters,
height × width × depth.

1. The Aperspectives

A Preliminary Remark

I look upon the Aperspectives as my first pictures–although I attempted this and that before them. They are not flashes of genius, but rather conceptions evolved over (long) years of work and then time after time discarded. If, for once, a conception became a draft and then even advanced as far as execution, that was still not the end but rather the beginning of a new and (at least in my eyes) improved version. Notwithstanding the long approach it records, this chapter is the shortest. And the only one that I regard as terminated.

The Starting Point

Initially I took my line from Zurich concrete art. In Zurich, artists–after the craziest of all wars–created something constructive (the word is to be taken literally). Along my path I came to another signpost: the books of Jean Gebser. He describes the present as the "aperspective" age and supports this argument with evidence drawn first and foremost from every branch of science. In the center stands Einstein's Theory of Relativity; the notion that the universe is limited and endless at one and the same time. Knowing nothing about physics, I was naive enough to take Einstein at his word, as it were, and to transfer it to art.

The Idea

The Aperspectives are, it is true, limited by their plane surface but at the same time endless: because this surface consists of segments which can be displaced cyclically to form continuously new patterns. The picture is never absolute but only relative in its finality. It comprises constants and variables, the formula being constant and its coordinates variable–again according to Einstein. It can also be looked at in this way: within its plane surface the Aperspective is nothing but the aspect, the phase of an imaginary movement, this movement being capable of completion by the beholder at any time.

The Realization

Typical example: Aperspective 1, page 64. It consists of a black ground on which twelve segments are secured by magnets. To alter the arrangement, the segments are picked up and placed in a different position. In their initial position all together form an endless movement, of which each individual segment contains a part. *Infinite* is to be interpreted thus: if segments are removed from the right-hand edge of the surface and joined again at the left, the movement continues–in the form of a sine curve–without interruption (Figures 1 through 5). Similarly top/bottom. The multiplicity of aspects comes more especially into evidence if the movement is not executed continuously but discontinuously (Figures 6 through 10).

The Beginnings

There are several variants of Aperspective 1, the earliest dating from 1952 and now lost. The extant version dates from 1956. I wrote an explanatory comment on Aperspective 3 (*Spirale* 5, Bern, 1955). First exhibition: 1957 at the Club Bel Etage, Zurich (numbers 1 and 3 are illustrated in the catalog). Incidentally, Aperspective 2 was a (likewise lost) sculpture (published in *Spirale* 4, Bern, 1954.)

There was also an Aperspective 4: an object with panes of glass arranged one behind the other with colors applied transparently (likewise lost).

Later I changed the name of the Aperspectives (borrowed, of course, from Gebser). Today they are called, somewhat more objectively, The Endless Spiral at a Right Angle (number 1) and The Large Sliding Mirror Picture (number 3).

A Postscript

The number of leads contained in the Aperspectives is in inverse proportion to the brevity of the chapter, and they are followed up only in the following chapters. Taken singly: the logicality of the concept (later–borrowing from music–I said: the seriality), the alterability, the principle of participation (the partnership between art producer and consumer), the primacy of the idea over the execution–and stemming therefrom: multiplication (production also being one aspect of seriality). Finally the question of distribution; for assuming these objects were made in large numbers, where should they be sold?

Aperspective 1

(The Endless Spiral at a Right Angle)
1952-1956
Acrylic lacquer on acrylic panels
Alterable elements with magnetic backs
900 × 540

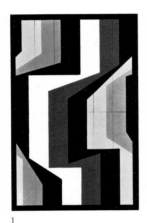

1

2

3

4

5

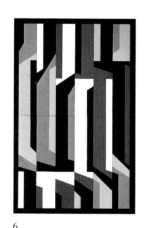 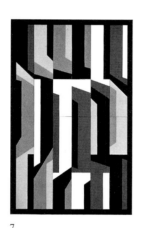 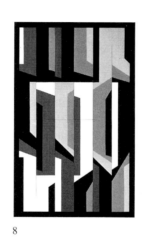 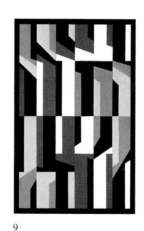 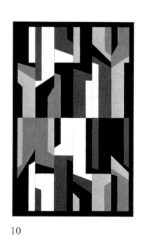

6   7   8   9   10

1

3

5

2

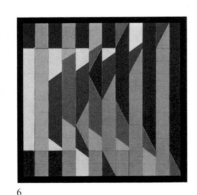

4

6

Aperspective 3

(The Large Sliding Mirror Picture)
1953/55
Explanatory comments on an experiment
in an alterable serial composition

The formal process of composition is based on a movement which is going on continuously. Endless: at the end of the picture plane the movement invariably returns to its beginning. It is divided on the basic grid into vertical mobile segments, twelve of which form one serial unit (Figures 1 and 2).

The segments are placed in the hands of the beholder. He himself executes the movement and allows a phase to persist as composition. However, continuous change is only one kind of arrangement conceivable, in practice the possibilities inherent in it are unlimited. Some of them are reproduced here within one unit (Figures 3 through 6).

The series is the result of several correlated units. The series in its entirety results from the sequence of the colors. That is to say, the movement returns to itself linearly within one unit, as does the color movement after the series has been run through (Figure 7).

The color series has no final and binding form. It is pattern only and its actual configuration resides in its changeability.

This does not mean that the series as a composition is merely the fortuitous sum of its individual elements. Each new pattern as a whole, as something that can be seen at one and the same time, must conform to an inner arithmetical law.

The aim of the experiment is to enable the beholder to be not only passively (as the contemplative onlooker) but also actively engaged in the process of the picture. In other words: although the picture is an object, it is not a completed fact from the subjective world of the artist. It needs the cooperation of the beholder and establishes the dialogue between him and the world of the object.

Or put still another way: it makes possible play in the ultimate sense of the word.

(From Spirale *5, Bern, 1955)*

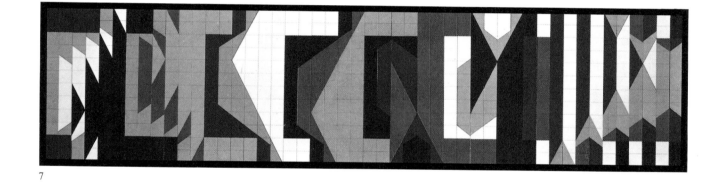

7

67

2. The Serial Pictures

A Preliminary Remark

Max Bill once wrote to the effect that he was seeking to convert thought itself into sensation–directly through a visual work, without words. To be exact, he said: "Art can mediate thought in such a way that the thought is directly perceivable information." I can still subscribe to this postulate without reservation (see "Conception-Perception; Fifteen Reflections on a Proposition of Max Bill," page 29). As regards method I had gone my own way–even at that time.

When I analyzed the pictures by Bill and his Zurich friends (in *Cold Art?*; Teufen, 1957), one thing struck me: that the formal structure was always readily intelligible and logical, but did not correlate with the structure of the color. In other words, form and color formed two different systems with the second serving to mark the first. (This is not an evaluative judgment but a statement. It is, moreover, a universal principle–I call it the "topological," which is to be seen throughout the history of art, for instance, in Gothic: see "The Color-Form Continuum," page 190.)

The Starting Point

I wanted to make constructive pictures on a different principle, which I call the "typological" (this is also a universal principle, appearing, for instance, in Baroque art). According to this, color and form make a structural unit.

The Idea

I based the pictures on "series"–similar to the serial technique in music–which comprise the parameters "form" and "color" as a unit–"form" here meaning not a quality (the "configuration"), but a quantity (the "proportion"). I tried out arithmetic series–proportions involving equal intervals in terms of figures, colors of equal gradations in terms of feeling and also geometric series–proportions and colors of progressive intervals and gradations in terms of figures and feeling, respectively. The progression consisted chiefly in doubling (1, 2, 4, 8...), and its division through the root of 2. The Golden Section also occurs; for example, in the Golden-sectioned Pillar, in homage to Le Corbusier for his Modulor (see pages 76 and 77).

An Intermediate Remark

A problem in all these experiments was: the proportions can be expressed *clare et distincte* but I did not see at that time a possibility of realizing color relations with the same precision. Proportions are numbers, colors are sensations. This is ultimately the problem of the measurability of color, ultimately a question of psychology. From my viewpoint–that of the artist–I have set down on paper a few reflections on some matters of principle (in "Bilder machen heute," *Spirale* 8, Bern, 1960).

The Realization

Typical example: Uncolored Series, pages 84 and 85. They consist of 63 bars which are fixed in a frame. Sixty-three is the sum of 1, 2, 4, 8, 16, 32, a numerical progression which is identical with the color gradation of white to black. At the same time the gradation of the brightness values decreases proportionally as the quantity increases. That is to say: the greatest step is between 1 and 2, the smallest between 16 and 32.

The Uncolored Series are changeable. The Cyclic Permutations and the Finite-Infinite Series (renamed Progressive Penetration), both of which are cycles, represent phases of a change which are fixed on the principle of the preeminent case. Another example is provided by the Room-wall Pictures: in these it is not the picture that changes but the beholder–or his point of view.

The Beginnings

The chapter did not begin with the consistent application of the serial technique. At first the Serial Pictures were round panels, like the Dark-Light Concentrum, derived from a geometrical black-white series, 1955. Shortly after followed the Yellow (Red/Blue) Excentrum, derived from complex color fields, and the Tangential Excentrum. The first Serial Picture in the true sense of the word was the 31 × 31-part Superangle, 1956 (renamed Diagon 31²); in the same year followed The Golden-sectioned Pillar. All these works were exhibited in the Club Bel Etage 1957, Zurich (illustrated in the catalog).

There then came the most lapidary versions of the serial idea: The Uncolored Series (in *DU* 8; Zurich, 1959), and the Colored Series. The latter also exist as multiples (in Daniel Spoerri's Edition MAT; exhibited in "Kinetische Kunst," Museum of Applied Arts, Zurich, 1960). An initial version of the Room-wall Pictures dates from 1956 (as a 1:1 model for the Swiss pavilion at the Triennale di Milano); a second version (1:10 model) is published in *Spirale* 8; Bern, 1960. The cycle Finite-Infinite Series is contained as a project in the catalog to the exhibition at Suzanne Bollag, Zurich, 1961.

Dark-Light Concentrum

1955/1956
Baked enamel on aluminum
Diameter: 534
Alterable
Markus Kutter collection, Basel

Pages 72, 73
Tangential Excentrum

1956/1957
Baked enamel on aluminum
Diameter: 600
Alterable, nine configurations

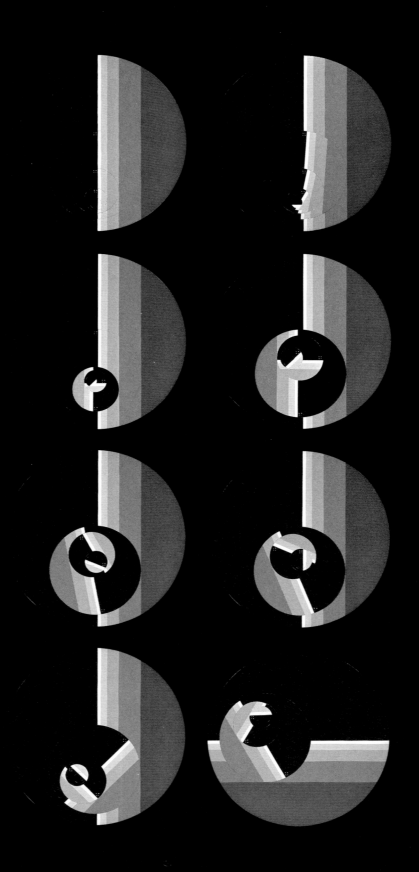

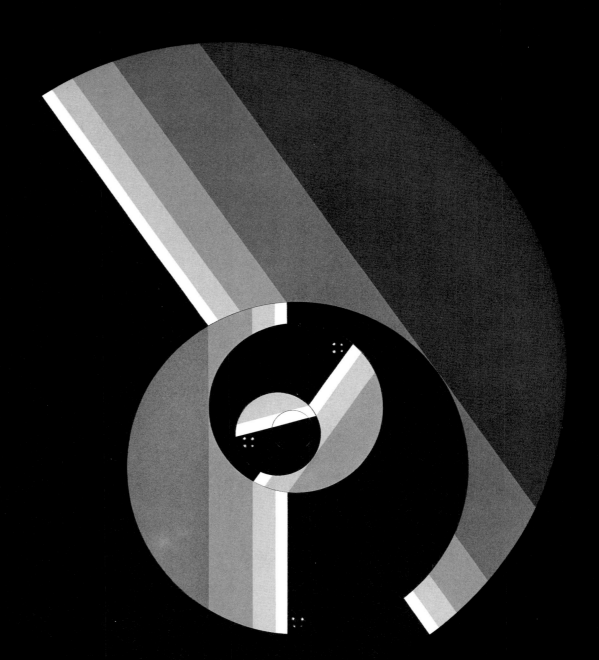

Yellow Excentrum

1956
Baked enamel on aluminum
Diameter: 534
Alterable
Enzo Mari collection, Milan

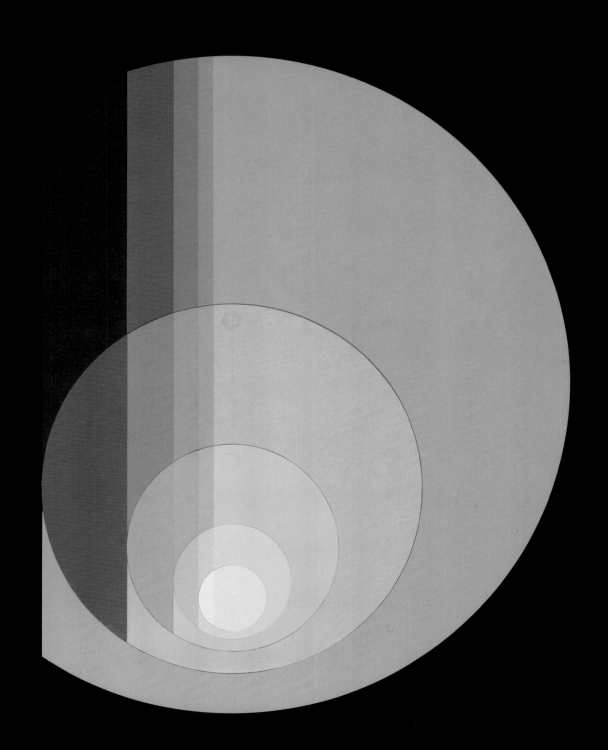

75

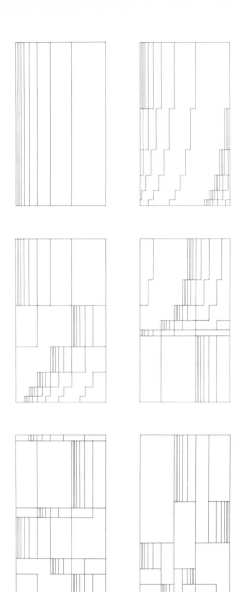

The Golden-sectioned Pillar

Alterable object, 1956/57
Baked enamel on aluminum
Height 1830, diameter 120

The Golden-sectioned Pillar is a homage to Le Corbusier, for his Modulor.

The Modulor is a new, human measure to replace the meter. It is based on the height of the solar plexus of a man of average size: 113 cm. This measure is divided or extended upward and downward in the ratio of the Golden Section.

The Golden Section, a proportion expressed by the formula $a: b = b: (a + b)$, creates a greaty variety of relations, which Le Corbusier uses for a more human, i.e., a more harmonious architecture.

The Golden-sectioned Pillar does not embody solely the proportions and system of the Modulor: it is alterable and in this way exemplifies the wealth of its possible combinations.

Figures 1 through 6 show rolled-out versions of the pillar-cylinder arranged in conformity with certain possible principles.

(*From "Bilder machen heute,"* Spirale *8, Bern, 1960*)

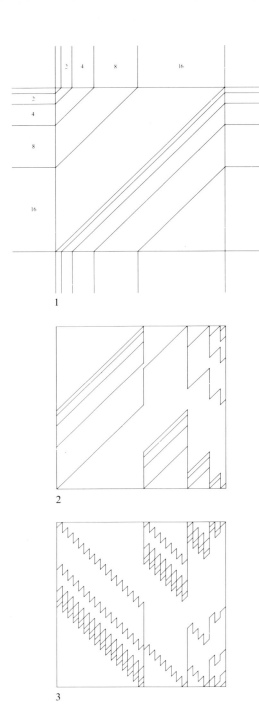

1

2

3

Diagon 31², Red/Green

Alterable object, 1956
Nitrocellulose on aluminum sections
620 × 620 mm

Diagon 31² consists of 31 bars, with diagonal stripes; the stripes are in the ratio 1-2-4-8-16 = 31 again (Figure 1).

The stripes form a cyclic permutation, i.e. they connect above/below and left/right without interruption.

The bars are to be displaced one at a time; in Figure 2 they are arranged backward, again in the ratio 16-8-4-2-1.

In Figure 3 the rods are also each turned through 180 degrees.

The color gradations have the same proportions as the stripes: 1-2-4-8-16. That is to say, each color gradation is twice as big as the previous one. And between the largest and smallest gradation there is again a cyclic ratio: the two colors are complementary.

The cycle is clearly shown in the diagram in Figure 4: a 31-part color circle in which color shades 1-2-4-8-16 are occupied, the progression of the color gradations being in inverse proportion to the stripes. That is to say, the broadest stripe (= ratio 16) = color shade 1; the narrowest stripe (= ratio 1) = color shade 16.

(From the prospectus for the edition of the Galerie Der Spiegel, Cologne, 1968)

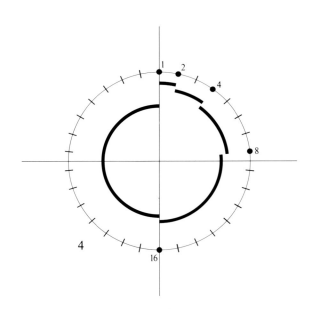

4

Progressive Penetration

1960
Nitrocellulose on aluminum
Each 630 × 630
Pierburg collection, Neuss, West Germany

Pages 82, 83
Progressive Penetration

(Finite-Infinite Series)
1960
Nitrocellulose on aluminum
Each made from a 630 × 630 square
Pierburg collection, Neuss, West Germany

Pages 84, 85
Uncolored Series

(Light-Dark Progression)
1956-1957
Printer's ink on plastic
Alterable, two configurations
Each 630 × 630

Pages 86, 87
Cyclic Permutation VA/VB

Diptych
1976
Nitrocellulose on aluminum
Each 685 × 685

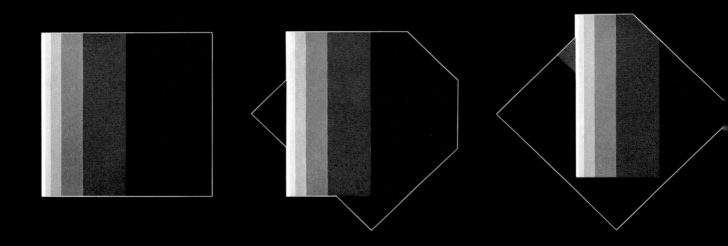

3. The Carro Pictures

The Starting Point

The serial technique is linear in principle, one-dimensional, and for this reason it is particularly suitable as a method for music, which proceeds linearly in time. In picture-making this characteristic imposes a limitation in principle. For my next step I wanted to retain the result of the serial technique–the integration of color and proportions–but I asked myself whether it would not be possible to extend it to a surface. A kind of field technique.

The Idea

It is as easy to describe as it is banal. While the serial pictures–as the name implies–are made up of series which run from one end to the other, one-dimensionally, that is, the Carro Pictures consist of squares (*carrés*) which are to be arranged in two dimensions.

The Realization

A typical example: Carro 64, page 92. The picture consists of a color series of 16 elements in sets of four (= 64). The first color series is arranged initially in a 4 × 4 square at random, or: the series, being folded on itself, coils into a spiral, allowing the elements to interpenetrate, and so forth. This 4 × 4 square is then–again by a random or symmetrical operation (by displacement, rotation, mirror-image formation)–passed through the other series to form Carro 64 and–if required–developed through additional operations. (Described in "Structure and Movement," in *Designing programmes*; Teufen, 1963).

In reality the individual Carros must be visualized as consisting of precision-made aluminum blocks like those used by printers for spacing type. They are placed in a chase (such as is also used in printing) which can be locked up mechanically or opened if the pattern is to be changed.

The Beginnings

The first sketches for the Carro Pictures were made in 1956, the first pictures in 1958: The Polychrome Monotone and Carro 64 were first exhibited, as prototypes, at Denise René, Paris, 1962 (and illustrated in the catalog).

Carro 64 was from the outset conceived as a participation object, as a multiple. The aim I had set myself was this: to design an object that, first, contained a broad spectrum of possible variations in conformity with a law–so that participation became really meaningful. And secondly; to design it for manufacture in large numbers and at a price everyone could afford (unlike my earlier objects, which were also intended for production in large numbers but would have been exorbitantly expensive).

On the assumption that the project would be implemented, I wanted to sell Carro 64–art as merchandise–to the stores. These initial plans came to nothing

until Daniel Spoerri brought out my first multiple in the Edition MAT (which, however, petered out in the usual commercial channels). A second attempt was made by Christian Holzäpfel (1962), the "large numbers" in this case running to 120 copies, which he distributed through the furniture trade (which sat on them). In 1965 George Staempfli sold a batch of the same size by mail order (no problem). There followed a Tokyo and a Genoa version.

A first move towards large-scale production was made in 1968 with the "do-it-yourself" version by Denise René and Hans Mayer. The total edition was three different color versions of 750 each.

Thanks to this undertaking I also obtained sufficient elements to take the Carro idea a stage further: there came into being cycles, angle Carros, double/triple/quadruple Carros–a whole Carro world (described in the prospectus for this edition).

A Postscript

Again in the case of the Carros I wanted to explore the parameter "relief": I wanted to apply the colors to Carros of heights that differed according to the gradations of the colors. I therefore had aluminum blocks machined to the required height–and was surprised by an entirely unexpected effect: each Carro reflected the light like a phonograph record, i.e., round the center point of the operation on the lathe.

I omitted the color and, thanks to this contribution by the lathe operator, I produced a series of Texture Pictures (first exhibited at George Staempfli, New York, 1965; illustrated in the catalog).

The idea of the Relief Pictures and the Relief Sculptures is also a spinoff of the Carro idea. (The Relief Pictures were first exhibited at George Staempfli, New York, 1967; and in the same year also at Ursula Brunner-Schwer in the Saba Studio, Villingen, where they were illustrated in the catalog).

Polychrome Monotone

1956/1958
Printer's ink on acryl resin squares
420 × 420 unframed
Alterable
Inge Gerstner-Höchberg collection, Basel

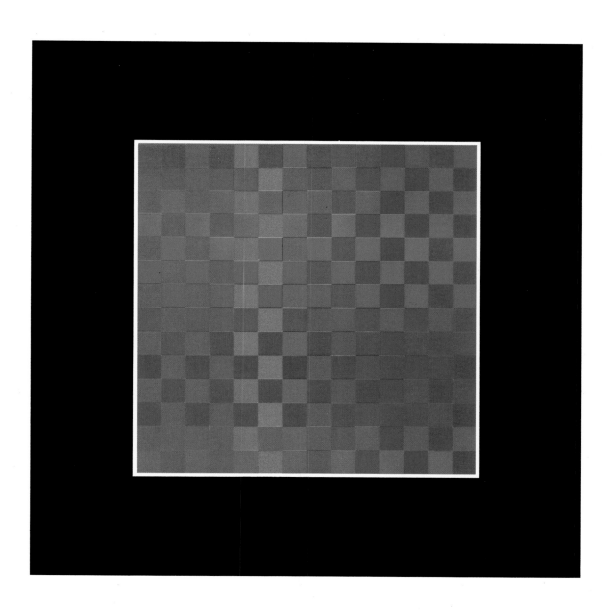

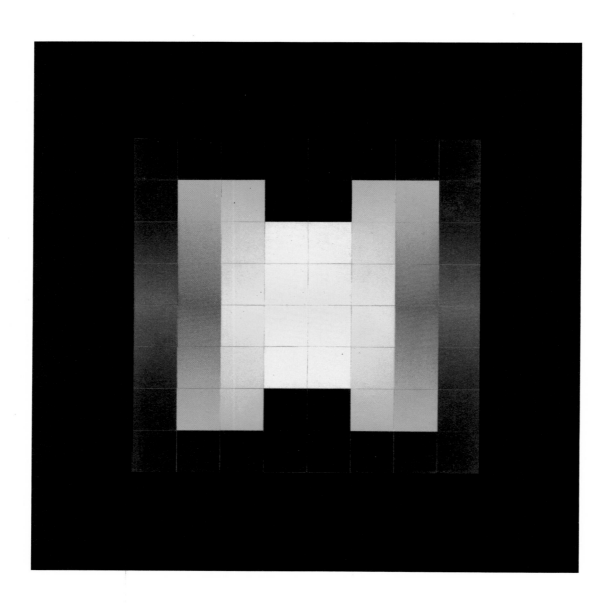

Carro 64

Alterable object, 1956/61
Edition Christian Holzäpfel KG, Ebhausen, 1962
Printer's ink on aluminum blocks

Carro 64 is a "do-it-yourself" picture–with almost unlimited possibilities: with only 16 of the 64 Carros there are 20,922,789,888,000 possible combinations (and at this point the mathematician stops calculating).

There are two ways of proceeding: at random and in conformity with a law. Most of the enormous number of combinations are produced at random; combinations in conformity with a law are reducible to a few symmetrical operations: displacement, rotation, and mirror-image formation.

An example for a mirror image: the 16 Carros (Figure 1) are arranged–at will–in a 4×4 square (Figure 2) and mirror images are formed on the horizontal (Figure 3) and the vertical axis (Figure 4).

The prospectus of the Staempfli Edition is reproduced on the two following pages. It shows some other possibilities, the technical function and the notation, according to the numbers on the individual Carros.

*(From "Think Program," catalog
to the exhibition at the Museum of Modern Art,
New York, 1973)*

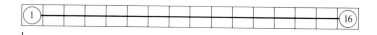

1

2

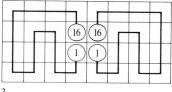

3

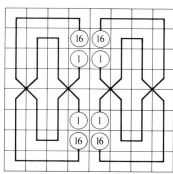

4

93

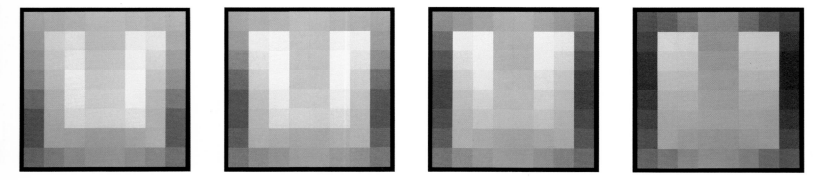

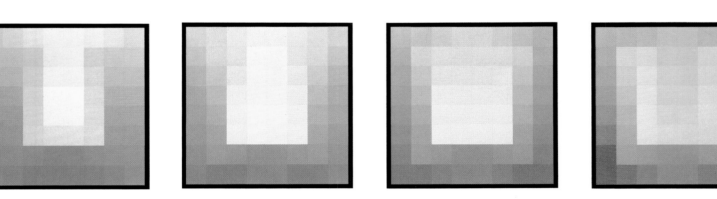

This picture is called Carro 64.

Here is the same picture in five of an unlimited number of versions:

Carro 64 is made of 64 accurately tooled aluminum cubes which are set in an adjustable white frame. The size is 16″ × 16″.

You can arrange and arrange and rearrange these colored cubes until you are satisfied. Only your taste and imagination limit the number of possible designs.

You get thousands of pictures by buying one, one of a limited edition of 120, issued by Staempfli Gallery. They are designed, numbered and signed by the Swiss artist Karl Gerstner. The price of each is $125. Are you interested? Order one from Staempfli Gallery, 47 East 77 Street, New York 21, N. Y.

First New York exhibition of Karl Gerstner's work at Staempfli Gallery,

February 2 to February 20, 1965

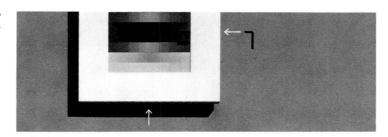

You release the tension in the frame with the attached key. One cube rises automatically.

Take all cubes out of the frame. You find that each carries a number from 1 to 16 which corresponds to its color shade. There are four identically numbered cubes to each shade.

It is best to arrange the cubes in front of you in four rows numbered in sequence. Place all numbers on the same side where you can see them.

You have completed your preparations and can begin to compose your picture.

Recipe 1

9	8	7	6	6	7	8	9
10	6	5	5	5	5	6	10
11	7	4	4	4	4	7	11
12	8	3	3	3	3	8	12
13	9	2	2	2	2	9	13
14	10	1	1	1	1	10	14
15	11	12	13	13	12	11	15
16	16	15	14	14	15	16	16

Recipe 2

13	12	5	4	4	5	12	13
14	11	6	3	3	6	11	14
15	10	7	2	2	7	10	15
16	9	8	1	1	8	9	16
16	9	8	1	1	8	9	16
15	10	7	2	2	7	10	15
14	11	6	3	3	6	11	14
13	12	5	4	4	5	12	13

Recipe 3

4	5	6	7	7	6	5	4
3	10	9	8	8	9	10	3
2	11	14	15	15	14	11	2
1	12	13	16	16	13	12	1
1	12	13	16	16	13	12	1
2	11	14	15	15	14	11	2
3	10	9	8	8	9	10	3
4	5	6	7	7	6	5	4

Recipe 4

8	16	6	16	4	16	2	16
15	7	15	5	15	3	15	1
8	14	6	14	4	14	2	14
13	7	13	5	13	3	13	1
8	12	6	12	4	12	2	12
11	7	11	5	11	3	11	1
8	10	6	10	4	10	2	10
9	7	9	5	9	3	9	1

Recipe 5

8	7	6	5	4	3	2	1
9	13	12	11	10	9	8	2
10	14	5	6	7	8	9	3
11	15	4	1	1	7	10	4
12	16	3	2	1	6	11	5
13	16	2	3	4	5	12	6
14	15	16	16	15	14	13	7
15	14	13	12	11	10	9	8

Here are five recipes which enable you to recreate the five pictures reproduced on the reverse page.

Of course you are now free to create your own compositions, ordered or disordered.

You can arrange the cubes either by preconception or mix them by accident.
The basic formula for Carro 64 foresees an almost unlimited number of ordered variants.

You can work out your solution with the cubes, or prepare them on paper.

Try to work with these recipes. Each contains a principle which can be varied at will.

Here are ten other recipes for further experimentation:

Recipe 6

5	6	7	8	9	10	11	12
4	11	10	9	8	7	6	13
3	12	15	16	1	2	5	14
2	13	14	16	1	3	4	15
2	13	14	16	1	3	4	15
3	12	15	16	1	2	5	14
4	11	10	9	8	7	6	13
5	6	7	8	9	10	11	12

Recipe 7

12	13	14	15	15	14	13	12
11	6	5	16	16	5	6	11
10	7	4	1	1	4	7	10
9	8	3	2	2	3	8	9
9	8	3	2	2	3	8	9
10	7	4	1	1	4	7	10
11	6	5	16	16	5	6	11
12	13	14	15	15	14	13	12

Recipe 8

14	15	14	15	2	3	2	3
13	16	13	16	1	4	1	4
14	15	14	15	2	3	2	3
13	16	13	16	1	4	1	4
12	9	12	9	8	5	8	5
11	10	11	10	7	6	7	6
12	9	12	9	8	5	8	5
11	10	11	10	7	6	7	6

Recipe 9

4	3	2	1	1	2	3	4
5	11	10	9	9	10	11	5
6	12	7	8	8	7	12	6
7	13	6	1	1	6	13	7
8	14	5	2	2	5	14	8
9	15	4	3	3	4	15	9
10	16	16	15	15	16	16	10
11	12	13	14	14	13	12	11

Recipe 10

1	4	14	3	15	2	16	1
16	13	11	6	12	5	13	4
2	5	7	8	10	7	11	14
15	12	10	9	9	8	6	3
3	6	8	9	9	10	12	15
14	11	7	10	8	7	5	2
4	13	5	12	6	11	13	16
1	16	2	15	3	14	4	1

Recipe 11

1	2	3	4	5	6	7	8
2	13	12	11	10	9	8	7
3	12	13	14	15	16	9	6
4	11	14	1	16	15	10	5
5	10	15	16	1	14	11	4
6	9	16	15	14	13	12	3
7	8	9	10	11	12	13	2
8	7	6	5	4	3	2	1

Recipe 12

5	4	3	2	2	3	4	5
6	7	8	1	1	8	7	6
11	10	9	16	16	9	10	11
12	13	14	15	15	14	13	12
12	13	14	15	15	14	13	12
11	10	9	16	16	9	10	11
6	7	8	1	1	8	7	6
5	4	3	2	2	3	4	5

Recipe 13

1	14	13	12	11	10	9	8
2	15	9	10	11	12	13	1
3	16	8	3	4	5	14	6
4	16	7	2	1	6	15	4
5	15	6	1	2	7	16	4
6	14	5	4	3	8	16	3
7	13	12	11	10	9	15	2
8	9	10	11	12	13	14	1

Recipe 14

1	5	2	5	3	5	4	5
16	12	16	11	16	10	16	9
1	6	2	6	3	6	4	6
15	12	15	11	15	10	15	9
1	7	2	7	3	7	4	7
14	12	14	11	14	10	14	9
1	8	2	8	3	8	4	8
13	12	13	11	13	10	13	9

Recipe 15

11	10	9	8	8	9	10	11
12	4	3	7	7	3	4	12
13	5	2	6	6	2	5	13
14	6	1	5	5	1	6	14
15	7	1	4	4	1	7	15
16	8	2	3	3	2	8	16
16	9	10	11	11	10	9	16
15	14	13	12	12	13	14	15

This is the recipe for the large picture reproduced on the reverse, in case you would like to come back to it.

Carro 64

Twenty-one part cycle
(Du Clair à l'Obscur à travers le Viol)
1960
Nitrocellulose on aluminum squares
Each 380 × 380

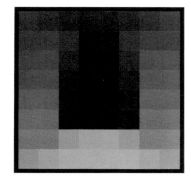

Carro 64 Doubles

1956-1958, 1968
Silkscreen on aluminum squares
Multiple
Edition Denise René/Hans Mayer, Paris/Krefeld
750 × 385

Carro 64 Angle

1956-1958, 1968
Silkscreen on aluminum squares
Multiple
Edition Denise René/Hans Mayer, Paris/Krefeld
385 × 385 × 385

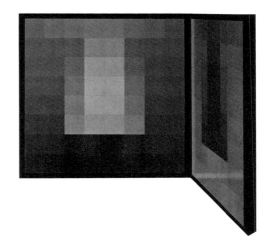

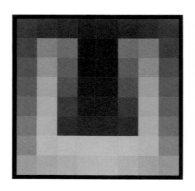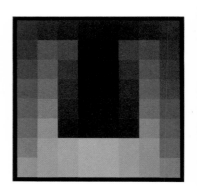

Purple Balance

(In Memory of Goethe)
1960/1980
Nitrocellulose on phenolic resin plates
Mounted in a slab of Gris de Lourdes marble
Each $720 \times 720 \times 180$

Color Relief 9

Cinnabar, Intro Version, 1966/1968
Nitrocellulose on masonite, 1640 × 1640 unframed
Dresdner Bank, Dortmund

106

Color Relief 10

Turquoise, Intro Version, 1966/1968
Nitrocellulose on masonite, 1640 × 1640 unframed
Dresdner Bank, Dortmund

107

Carro Texture 3

One picture lighted two ways, 1961/1964
Machined aluminum blocks, 720 × 720 framed
George Staempfli collection, New York

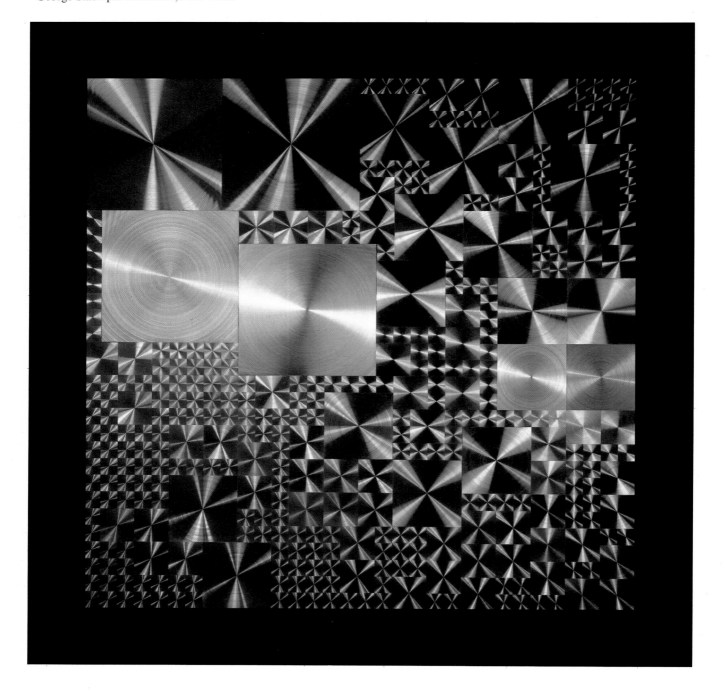

4. The Metachromes

The Starting Point

Work on the Aperspectives served to develop criteria. Work on the Serial Pictures and Carro Pictures gave my knowledge greater depth and breadth, particularly with regard to method. Now: how was the instrumentarium I had acquired to be used if I was to conceive it not as an end in itself but as an end to a higher purpose?

Incidental Remark

In J.O. Fleckenstein's biography of Leibniz I found the sentence which I will quote as the leitmotiv of this chapter (if not of the whole book): "Even if there is never knowledge of the absolute, there is absolute knowledge. The domain of this absolute knowledge is mathematics."

The Idea

"Metachrome" is a word coined from *metamorphosis* and *chroma*, meaning, therefore, color transformations. Previously these pictures were called Chromomorphoses. I changed their name because *meta* expresses the enigmatic and ambiguous more precisely.

The elements of constructive art – proportions, forms, colors–are analogous to mathematics and have to be precisely determined, like numbers and signs. I found (and still find) it particularly fascinating that precisely such an emotion-charged medium as color forms a logically coherent system; virtually inexhaustible in its nuances, clear and simple in its categories.

This and the additional fact that this system was discovered by an artist (Philipp Otto Runge), but never used for art prompted me to make inquiries; specifically, to go in search of absolute knowledge in this undiscovered country. The Metachromes are pictures each of which embodies a color phenomenon which is unique in nuance and prototypical in category.

A Second Incidental Remark

For the Metachromes I tried for the first time to use exact numerical ratios not only for the proportions but also for the color gradations, by weighing the paint on a precision balance. The procedure is comparatively simple if what is involved is a simple series, i.e., a series consisting of two colors; for example, black-white–and (so far) insuperably difficult if the effects of several colors are combined; the principal reason being that the material, the pigment, varies from shade to shade too much for the requisite homogeneity to be ensured qua numerical series.

I have not abandoned the goal and more recently I have made progress in terms not of the calculations but rather of the method. This persistence in attempting to have color as much under control as form is not an end in itself. Rather, experience shows that calculation is the best, indeed the only, means of capturing the image of a sensation with the desired accuracy. I was encouraged in these experiments by meeting (in spring 1980) Jakob Weder, who had been quietly researching this very problem for years.

The Realization

Typical example: "The warm/cold, pure/impure, light/dark violet," a tryptichon of nuances which are too delicate to be reproduced. The example is typical because here we have a very specific color which is to be transformed in conformity with the three possible categories: there are no others. Another example: Metachrome 3.22 is a tribute to Goethe, evidence in support of his speculative contention that white seen through a semiopaque medium produces yellow, but black seen through a semiopaque medium, on the contrary, produces blue (page 129).

The Beginnings

The first Metachromes were picture panels rolled up with printer's ink. They date from 1958 (Polychromy Accentuated in Blue, Gloor collection, Zurich) and were documented for the first time in *DU* 8, 1959 (Blue-Yellow Sequence via Red) and exhibited for the first time at Suzanne Bollag, Zurich. The first Metachrome sculpture was also to be seen there (Red-Green Color Body), followed by others like the Metachrome Janus Sculpture Blue/Red. Parallel to color transformations in steps there were also those proceeding in continuous sequences.

I also experimented with various textures, which I incorporated into the conception. For example, reflecting metal surfaces contrast with nonreflecting color surfaces, causing the picture to alter in appearance depending on the incidence of the light or the position of the beholder.

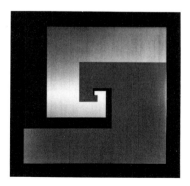

The Red-Green Double Square

1961
Printer's ink on aluminum
525 × 525 framed

Page 114
Four Times Gray

1960/1962
Printer's ink on aluminum
525 × 525 framed

Page 115
The Light-Dark Lilac

1960
Printer's ink on aluminum
525 × 525 framed, diagonal

Page 116
The Red-Red Diagon

1960
Printer's ink on aluminum
525 × 525 framed

112

Page 117
The Warm-Cold Blue

1961
Printer's ink on aluminum
525 × 525 framed, diagonal

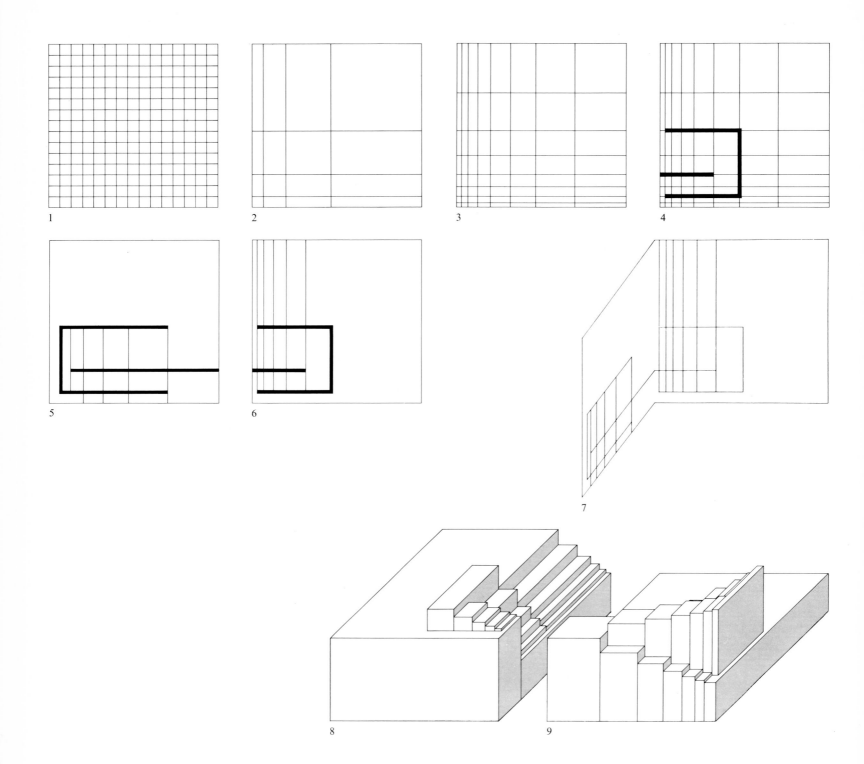

1 2 3 4

5 6

7

8 9

Directions for Making Pictures

1. A grid of squares of equal size
2. is structured in a ratio of 1:2; in
3. the structure obtained in 2 is divided geometrically, $\sqrt{2}$; in
4. the structure obtained in 3 is articulated; in
5. the structure for a Metachrome–a color transformation–is crystallized out; in
6. the basic structure is examined for other interpretations it may allow; in
7. the two structures 5 and 6 are combined to form a picture in an angled form; in
8. the same structures are explored for their plastic expression (see also pages 122 and 123)

The picture as the transformation of an idea; what is sought is the formula, the fixed point; the form is variable. I know where I am setting out from; I don't know where I shall arrive–surprise is the greatest pleasure in my work. Sometimes an idea expresses itself in the form of an open cross (Figure 10), another time in the form of a closed cube (Figure 11). From the idea of conceiving the color not as an applied surface but as a plastic, structural unit emerges the color relief.

(From "Bilder machen heute," Spirale *8, Bern, 1960.)*

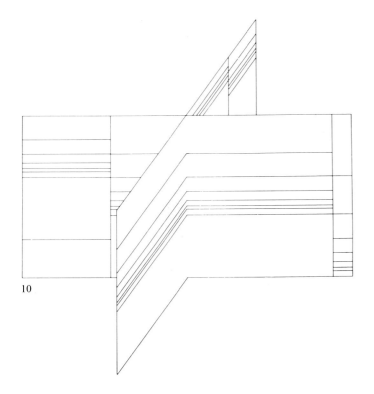

10

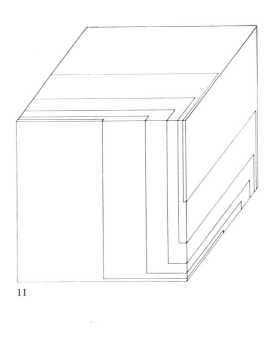

11

The Gray-Red Progression on Green

1960/1961
Printer's ink on aluminum
525 × 525 framed

Pages 122, 123
Metachrome Sculpture, 2.05/2.06

1962/1976
Nitrocellulose on phenolic resin plates
Floor diptych on Blanc-Calacta marble
Each 750 × 750 × 175

Pages 124, 125
Metachrome Diptych 1.01/1.02

1959/1960
Nitrocellulose on aluminum
Each 632 × 622
Wilhelm Zilling collection, Neuss, West Germany

123

Metachrome 4.03

1958/1960
Nitrocellulose on aluminum
1235 × 812
Mia Zürcher collection, Zurich

Page 128
Metachrome 4.05

1958/1960
Nitrocellulose on aluminum
927 × 618

Page 129
Metachrome 3.22

(In Memory of Goethe)
1958/1960
Nitrocellulose on aluminum
1235 × 812

Pages 130, 131
Metachrome Janus Sculpture Blue/Red

1958/1974
Nitrocellulose on phenolic resin plates
1125 × 685 × 168 without base
Hanns-Dieter Herrmann collection, Karlsruhe

5. The Apparatus

The Starting Point

I had previously tried to bring as many parameters as possible into the basic idea of a picture. These efforts received–in the early sixties–a new impetus from the activity of friends; mainly from the Parisian Groupe de Recherche d'Art Visuel. Le Parc and Morellet in particular stimulated the zest for experiment. The aim: to try out previously developed methods on new materials and in new techniques. Under the heading Apparatus are subsumed groups of studies whose common characteristic is, as I have said, that peculiar to apparatus which–subject to qualification–I would call the programming of time. Subject to qualification, because all pictures which are alterable imply by that very fact the parameter of time (i.e., most of those produced before the Apparatus).

In other respects the individual groups of apparatus are heterogeneous:

Prism Pictures
Lens Pictures
Auto Vision
E-Motion Pictures
Times Square
Color Organ

I no longer follow the pattern of the other chapters but simply provide the text for each of the illustrations–but once again with an exception, namely the Color Curtain, of which no illustration–apart from a model–exists.

Color Curtain

Twenty-two triangular bars are arranged vertically in a frame measuring 300×226 cm. Each side of the triangle is a different color; the triangle sides in combination form at any time a homogeneous color series. The bars are pivoted at the top and bottom and can be turned through 60 degrees at a time. The rotation is triggered by an impulse from a programmer.

In the effect produced the colors are mixed, continuously or discontinuously, depending on the program; the color is set in motion–virtually and actually. (Exhibited for the first and last time: documenta 4, Kassel, 1968.)

An Additional Remark

The features the pictures have in common are not accounted for solely by the themes of the separate chapters (or vice versa); there are also common characteristics impinging, as it were, laterally. For instance, texture, the character of the surface, plays a role throughout. Or–and this is what I want to speak of here–the phenomenon by which color can be created without colors.

In the Prism Pictures color is generated by prismatic refraction; likewise in the Lens Pictures. In the Tension Pictures color is made visible by the polarization of light: through filters which let a specific spectrum pass through a transparent sheet depending on the tensions in the material. The E-Motion Pictures produce color by rotation of a physiological kind: the rotation of black-white propellers produces a color effect in the eye. But research of this kind is evident not only in various sub-chapters of "Apparatus" but also in other chapters, for example, among the Carro Texture Pictures, the production of color through refraction of light in the grooves left in the Carros after machining (pages 108 and 109).

Prism Picture

Alterable object, 1958-1962
Plexiglas block with prism facets
Colored fluorescent light
720 × 720
Robert Sarnoff collection, New York

Prism-shaped grooves (i.e., V-shaped incisions at an angle of 60 degrees) are milled along and across a square block of Plexiglas. From all four sides colored light is directed into the block and reflected and refracted by the prisms. The color of the light can be altered on each side and mixed as desired in the prisms. (First exhibited at the Galerie Denise René, Paris, 1962, illustrated in the catalog.)

Lens Picture

Alterable object, 1962-1964
Plexiglas lens with photoreproduction
Fluorescent light
720 × 720
Albright-Knox Art Gallery, Buffalo, New York

Concentric, black-and-white circles are viewed through a lens (a kind of outsize magnifying glass). This lens is shaped on a lathe from Plexiglas and has a special wave-shaped profile. It has a twofold effect on the drawing placed under it: first, color is produced by the refraction of light on the black-and-white edges of the circles: specifically red/green on the concave and blue/yellow on the convex curves of the lens. Second, the intrinsic geometric pattern is continuously deformed depending on the position of the beholder. See also overleaf. (First exhibited at the Gallery abc, Winterthur, 1964; illustrated in the invitation.)

Pages 138, 139
Magenta-Turquoise Lens Picture

1962-1964
Plexiglas lens with one-of-on-kind silkscreen
Fluorescent light
720 × 720 mm
Rotraut Tanner collection, Dornach, CH

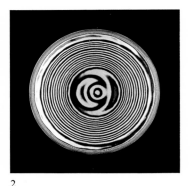

1

2

3

4

136

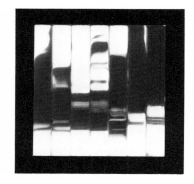

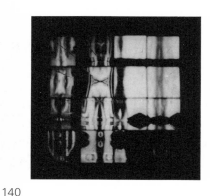

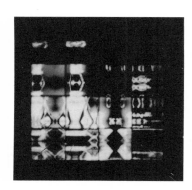

140

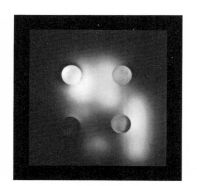

Auto Vision

Performance object, 1963
Black-and-white television set with seven different scopes
540 × 615 × 340 without base

The name underlines the difference from television: it denotes not the transmission of programs but the immediate generation of programs. Normal television programs are abstracted through a scope and made so unrecognizable that they become nonrepresentational.

From top to bottom the illustrations each show two moments through the cylindrical scope, the kaleidoscope, the opaque reflector, and the concentric prisms. (First exhibited in: Haus am Lützowplatz, Berlin, 1964. There were in one room thirteen TV sets all showing the same program but in each case transformed in a different way).

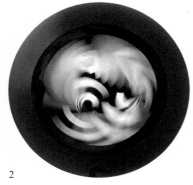

1

2

Atmos-Sphere

(E-Motion Picture)
Performance object, 1964-1967
Plexiglas sphere with rotating propellers
Nitrocellulose on phenolic resin plates
Neon light
1660 mm with base, diameter of sphere 800 mm

The name E-Motion Picture comes from the fact that a performance is given as if in the cinema, namely, by means of color and movement sensations.

Against a black ground are arranged three sets of propellers which are black/white on one side and graded in color on the other. The propeller sets can be adjusted at will and set in motion; first, they rotate at various speeds in relation to each other; second, they all rotate together on a common disk. The speed of the disk can be regulated; the higher it is, the more psychedelic the effect produced. (First exhibited at the Gallery George Staempfli, New York, 1967; illustrated in the catalog.)

Figure 1 shows the Atmos-Sphere in a stationary position; Figure 2 at high speed.

142

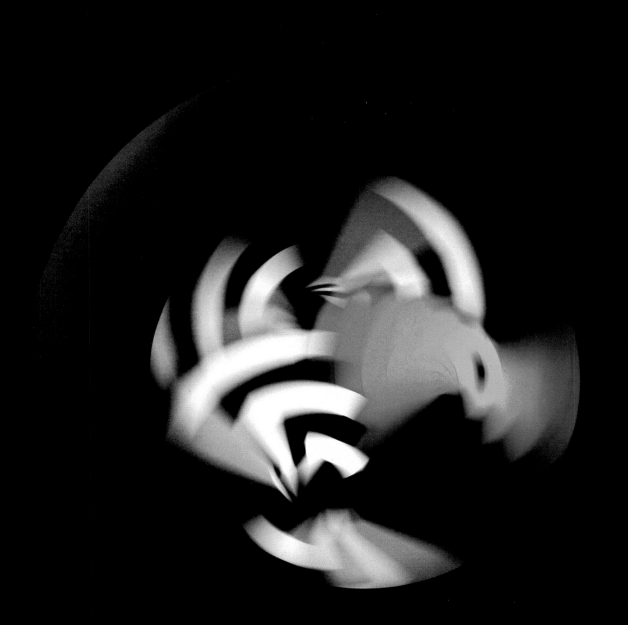

Times Square

Performance object, 1965
530 different colored lamps and programmer
1200 × 1200
Galerie Denise René, Paris

On the one hand the name comes from Times Square in New York, on the other hand it denotes the transformation of what it means literally: a spectacle takes place in time on a square.

A black backing holds 530 electric filament bulbs on a regular grid. These bulbs are arranged in 22 square groups, which are of various sizes and interlock with each other. Each of these groups has its own color; together they form a colored continuum from inside outward or vice versa; each is connected to its own circuit and is generated–using a punch card–by a programmer. There are 12 different programs for each Times Square. (First exhibited in the Op-Art Galerie, Esslingen, 1966.)

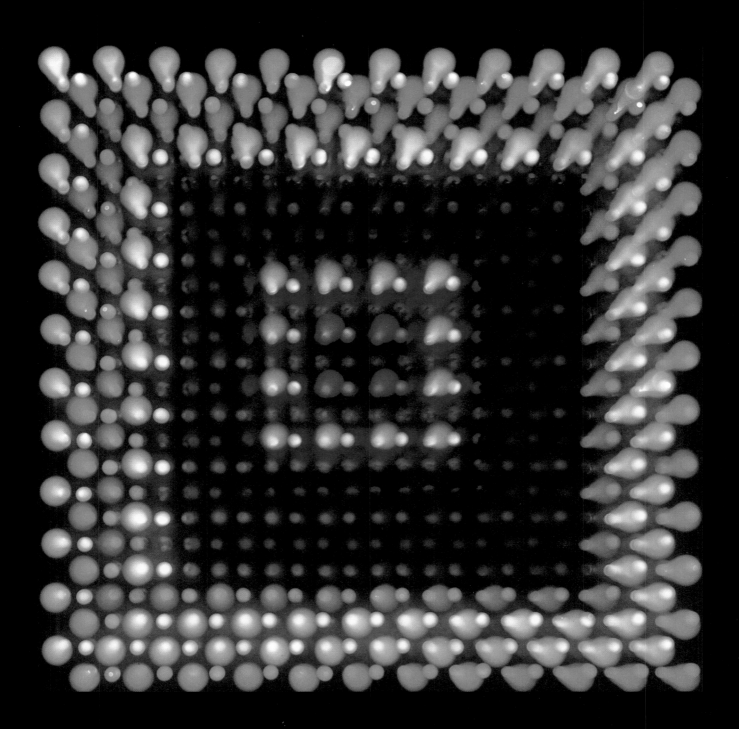

145

Color Organ

Environmental object, 1960-1969
48 Plexiglas spheres with light of various colors
generated through a sound-light apparatus
Approx. $4000 \times 4000 \times 2000$

Since the French Jesuit Louis Bernard Castel invented the *clavecin oculaire*, or color piano, about 1725 there have been repeated attempts to "perform" colors and sounds at the same time.

Castel's instrument consisted of two disks which could be turned on a common axis at different speeds. Depression of a key on the keyboard caused the color on the front disk corresponding to the note to appear in the cutout of the apparatus; the rear disk was divided into twelve segments (like the twelve semitones of the tempered octave) and formed the "melodic" and the "harmonic" colors as parts of concentric rings (from Alexander Laszlo, *Die Farbenlichtmusik*; Leipzig, 1925).

I have never seen or heard the color piano. But I cannot imagine that the effect on the eye is comparable in quality with that on the ear; the tones involve me as the listener immediately, the reception of the colors as envisaged by Castel represents rather an intellectual pleasure if any at all.

The problem that I pondered over originally has been largely overtaken by the disco culture: how can tones and colors be conveyed with the same emotional intensity?

One should be as filled with visual as with auditory impressions. For this reason I started with the idea of the organ rather than of the piano: no other instrument has the same physical/psychical potency. And so that there was no perception *à distance*, I designed the Color Organ in the form of a cave: tones and colors (more exactly, colored lights) should impinge on the beholder/listener from all sides.

Forty-eight spheres of white Plexiglas, each 60 cm in diameter, hang from the ceiling in a pattern of mirror symmetry and are reflected in a mirror on the floor. In the spheres there are–divided equally between the two halves of the symmetrical pattern–2×24 filament lamps of different colors. These lamps light up according to the music. Frequency corresponds to color shade, and the audible range of frequencies (= Hertz) is divided into as many parts as the Color Organ has spheres. Volume corresponds to light intensity; i.e., the sphere lights up brightly for a loud note and weakly for a soft note. (Created for an exhibition at the Kaufhof Dortmund, 1969; later shown at the exhibition "Freunde, Fruend, Friends," at the Kunsthallen in Bern and Düsseldorf, 1969.)

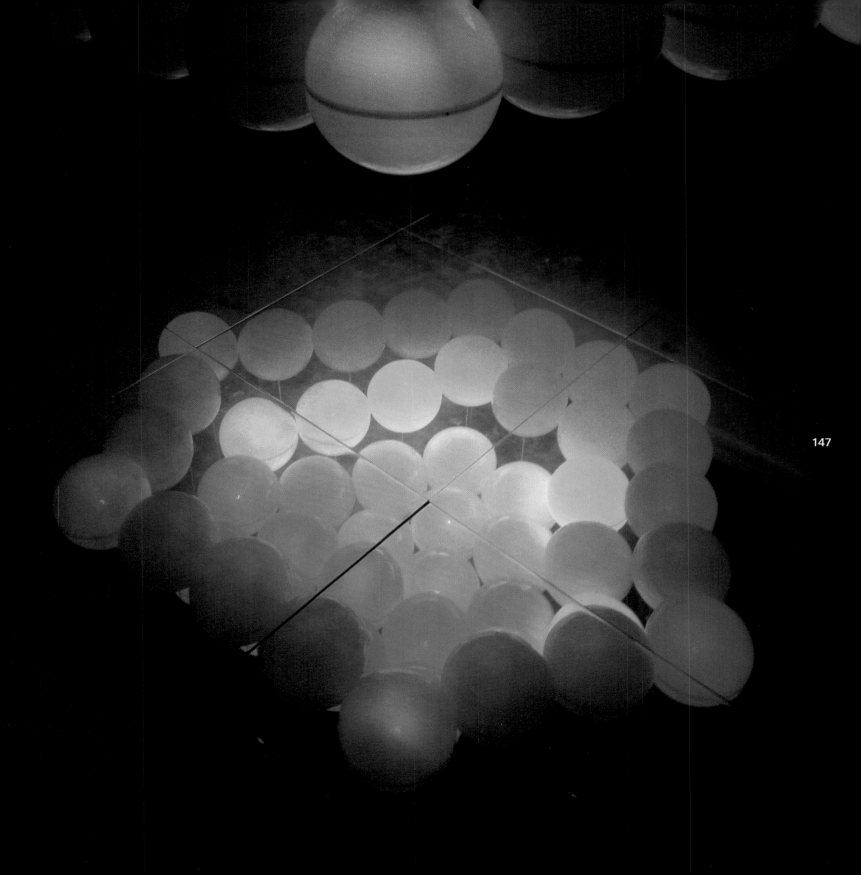

147

6. The AlgoRhythms

A Preliminary Remark

The apparatus cost a great deal of time and money, for one thing; for another they were extraordinary trouble-prone as exhibits. The programmer for Times Square went down after a few minutes in New York–although I had transformed the voltage correctly, I did not know that I also had to adjust the phase. And so on. The main reason why, for all the pleasure experimenting gave me, I came to lose my zest for it is no doubt that I realized I would never attain the standard of technology necessary to transform my ideas adequately. I say this with a certain regret because laser techniques would be just the thing to open up (A)perspectives.

The Starting Point

I wanted to use only a technique which I knew I could handle. But the project which I had been turning over in my mind for some time was presumptuous on another count. It involved nothing less than the total picture. Total because it should include, qua combinatory theory, all conceivable pictures (qualification: constructive pictures). To this end I had designed a morphological box with all the already proven parameters and all the others that should supplement and complete these (including the appurtenant elements)–a Mendeleev system of visual elements.

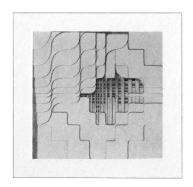

The Idea

When work on the project started to be serious, its dimensions also shrank to a more manageable size. The result distilled more and more to an alternative to the Carro idea. There the whole point had been the programming of color structures and here it was to be that of formal structure. When I had narrowed the idea down in this way, I discovered circular structures of a highly symmetrical regularity from which other forms, including asymmetrical ones, could be derived at will. The interesting point about them is that these forms always fit together precisely. In whatever sequence they are superposed, however they are rotated and reversed, the segments of the circles invariably touch each other and run into each other at 0 degrees. This also provides the name: AlgoRhythm is an altered form of algorithm, or a special process for solving a certain type of problem. (Described in *Do-it-yourself-Kunst*; Cologne, 1970.)

The fact that François Fricker provided a mathematical proof for my work (see page 152) gave me all the more pleasure in that I regard myself as being below average in mathematical ability.

The Realization

A typical example: AlgoRhythm 3, Edition Roche, Basel, page 154. It consists of five layers, i.e., five sheets out of each of which a shape has been stamped. These sheets are placed one on top of the other like a passe-partout. They are colored on one side in a scale of five different reds, and on the other in a scale of white to black.

The Beginnings

I can no longer assign an exact date to the original idea for the total picture; it may have originated in the mid-1960s. The first concrete drafts were produced in 1968; the first pictures were realized in 1969: AlgoRhythm 1, exhibited for the first time in Berlin in 1970, in the Haus am Lützowplatz (documented in the catalog).

In AlgoRhythm 1 for the first time I used colors by adaptation of the "Uniform Color Space" of Gunter Wyszecki of Ottawa, a fascinating system based on the latest scientific knowledge.

A Postscript

Perhaps no other object has ever run to so many copies as AlgoRhythm 3 and AlgoRhythm 4 (together over 100,000)–an irony of fate when I think that, by this time, I had long since shelved the idea of multiples. And yet there was a certain logic in the process, for none of my earlier objects had been so suitable–predestined, one might say–for multiplication. There is no original AlgoRhythm, nor can there be one–unless one of the billions of patterns is designated as such.

A Post-Postscript

After I had put this apodictic sentence to paper, I was immediately induced to refute it. There came into being series of reliefs, the AlgoOvals, which–as much to my surprise as to my joy–recalled the colored reliefs of the revered Jean Arp.

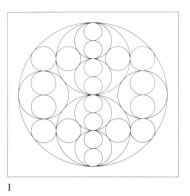

1

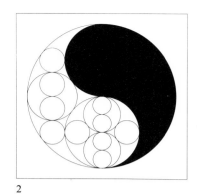

2

3

150

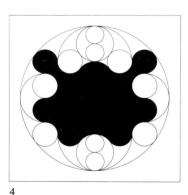

4

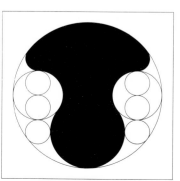

5

AlgoRhythm 1

Alterable object of 7 plates 1969-1970
Nitrocellulose on phenolic resin plates
810 × 800

Invitation to the unknown reader to make a picture for himself: an AlgoRhythm 1.

If you are not a handyman, don't hesitate to do as I do and find someone who is handier than you are. The do-it-yourself part should apply rather to the design than to the execution. Carry out the following steps:

1. Bring the construction, Figure 1, to the desired size.

2. Derive forms from along the construction lines; Figures 2 to 5 show four of the virtually unlimited number of possibilities.

3. Transfer the forms to paper (or a more solid material) and cut them out as a kind of passe-partout. Add colors–or textures–at discretion.

4. Place the passe-partouts one on top of the other any way you like so that they combine to make a picture. Reversing them is possible; likewise rotation, but only through 180 degrees.

5. Fix the separate parts: paste or lay in a frame.

(From: Do-it-yourself-Kunst,
Brevier für jedermann, *Spiegelschrift 3,
Köln, 1970)*

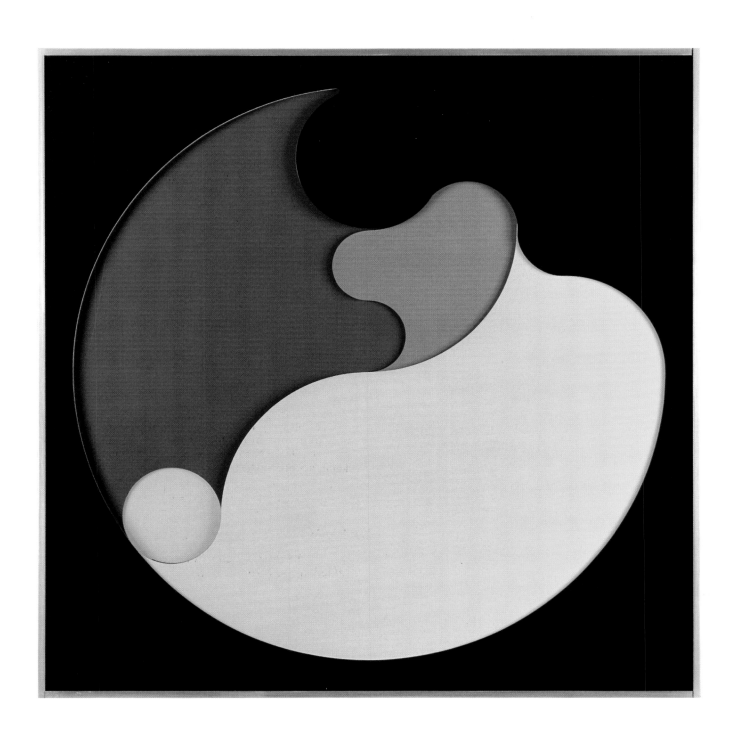

François Fricker:
A Surprising Characteristic
of Inscribed Circles

Dedicated to Karl Gerstner,
who discovered it

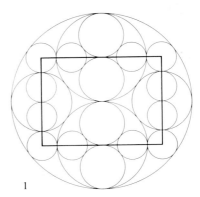

1

Figure 1 shows an excerpt from a figure drawn by Karl Gerstner [1, p. 78-79]. In this note the following surprising result is deduced: *The twelve "small circles" are all of equal size; moreover, their centers lie on the boundary of a rectangle.*

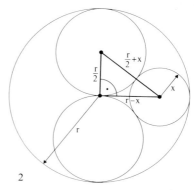

2

In the following I always refer to the radius of the initial circle as r. In my first step I determine the radius of the circle on the right in Figure 2. Let it be called x. Then, according to Pythagoras,

$$\left(\frac{r}{2}\right)^2 + (r-x)^2 = \left(\frac{r}{2} + x\right)^2;$$

therefore:
$$x = \frac{r}{3}.$$

Thus the radius of eight of the twelve circles mentioned above is shown to be r/6.

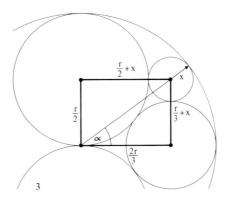

3

In a second step I determine the radius of the "small circle" in Figure 3. Let it again be called x. (N.B. The right angle in the center of this circle is still unknown.) The cosine law produces the two conditions:

$$\left(\frac{r}{3}+x\right)^2 = (r-x)^2 + \frac{4r^2}{9} - \frac{4r}{3}(r-x)\cos\alpha,$$

$$\left(\frac{r}{2}+x\right)^2 = (r-x)^2 + \frac{r^2}{4} - r(r-x)\sin\alpha.$$

This system is equivalent to

$$r-2x = (r-x)\cos\alpha,$$
$$r-3x = (r-x)\sin\alpha.$$

From which it follows that

$$(r-2x)^2 + (r-3x)^2 = (r-x)^2,$$

or again,

$$x = \frac{r}{6}.$$

Thus the twelve small circles in Figure 1 are in fact all of equal size. Moreover, the auxiliary quadrangle in Figure 3 now proves to be a rectangle (because the pairs of opposite sides are equal).

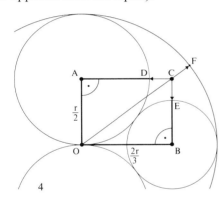

4

These arguments may be replaced by the following simpler proof: Let a rectangle first be drawn (Figure 4) and let it be shown that

$$\overline{CD} = \overline{CE} = \overline{CF} = \frac{r}{6}.$$

The procedure is thus:

$$\overline{CD} = \overline{AC} - \overline{AD} = \overline{OB} - \overline{AD} = \frac{2r}{3} - \frac{r}{2} = \frac{r}{6},$$

$$\overline{CE} = \overline{BC} - \overline{BE} = \overline{OA} - \overline{BE} = \frac{r}{2} - \frac{r}{3} = \frac{r}{6},$$

$$\overline{CF} = r - \overline{OC} = r - \sqrt{\overline{OB}^2 + \overline{BC}^2} =$$

$$r - \sqrt{\frac{4r^2}{9} + \frac{r^2}{4}} = r - \frac{5r}{6} = \frac{r}{6}.$$

[1] Karl Gerstner, Do-it-yourself-Kunst; Köln, 1970.

Addendum

It is immediately apparent from this argument that the rectangle in Figure 1 has sides of lengths r and 4r/3. From this two deductions may be made.

First, the twelve small circles may be supplemented to make fourteen circles of equal size in such a way that the long sides of the rectangle are now completely filled (Figure 5).

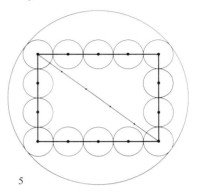

5

Second, the diagonals of the rectangle are 5r/3 in length and thus produce the Pythagorean number triple 3, 4, 5 (also Figure 5).

This number triple is also implicitly contained in Figure 2 and the sequences of thought following thereon (Figure 6).

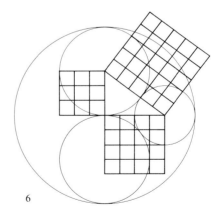

6

153

AlgoRhythm 3

1973
Multiple
Roche AG, Basel
Printed and
laminated cardboard
310 × 310

154

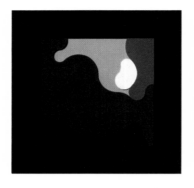 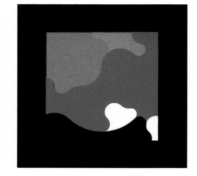

 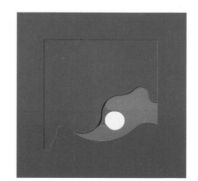

155

AlgoRhythm 7

Two versions
1974
Multiple, Edition Denise René/Hans Mayer, Paris/Krefeld
Printed and laminated cardboard
600 × 600

156

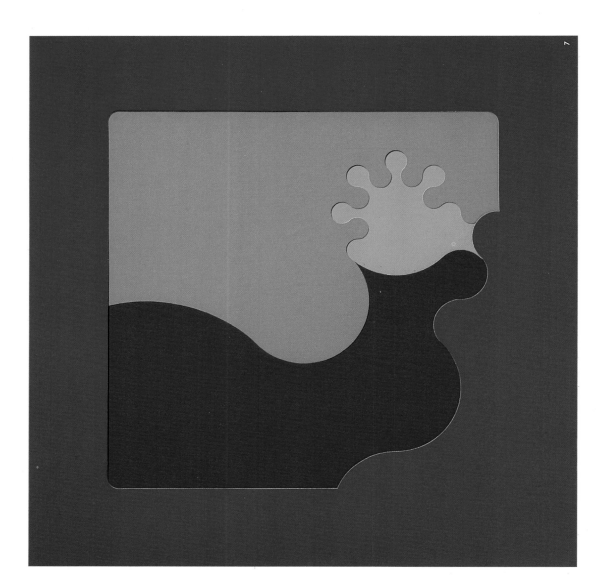

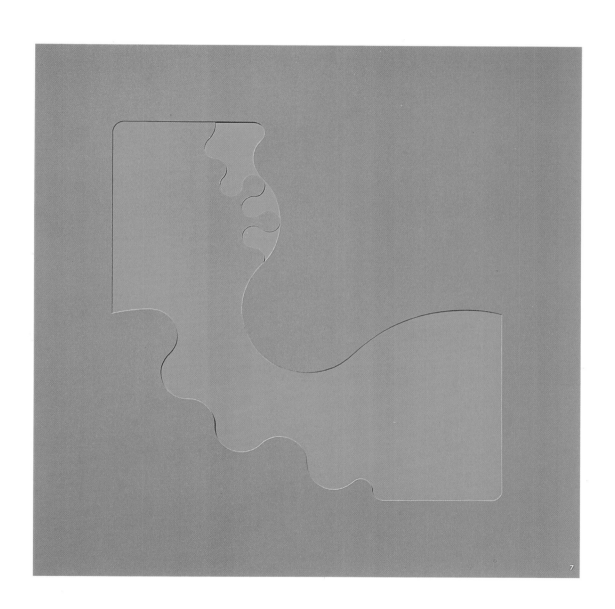

AlgoOval 1

1969-1970, 1979
Nitrocellulose on Mediapan
800 × 690

158

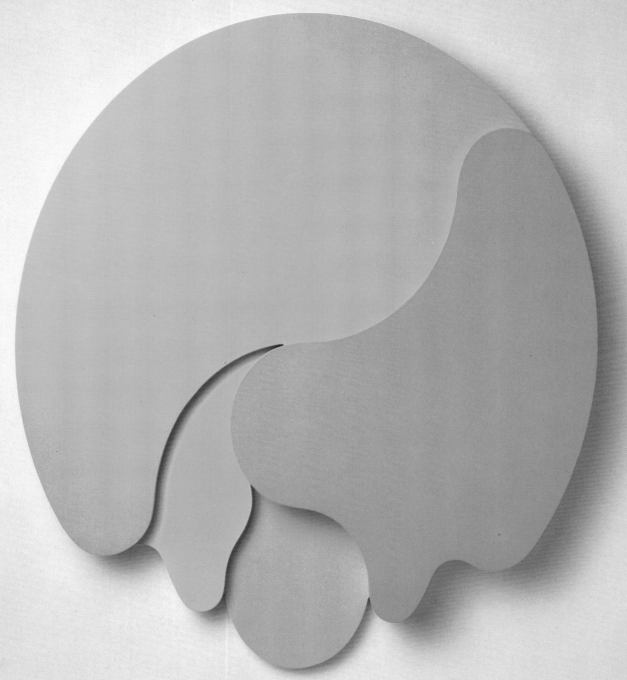

AlgoOval 4

1969-1970, 1979
Nitrocellulose on Mediapan
800 × 690

7. The Color Sounds

A Preliminary Remark

Even if the chapters follow one another in numerical order, this does not mean that the story is being told here in the order in which it fell out. Although the Color Sounds come after the AlgoRhythms chronologically, they follow the Color Reliefs formally (and these in turn proceeded from the Carro idea). As regards content the Color Sounds must be connected with the Metachromes.

The Starting Point

The Metachromes are pictures of a reality which exists only as a model: views from the universe of color. Albers (in his Homage to the Square) had a different starting point: he was interested in colors as a phenomenon; he explored their interaction more precisely than anyone else. With the Color Sounds (which are an "Homage to the Homage to the Square") I set my sights on a third target: the impact of color on the beholder.

In this way I wanted to approach a goal which I had already set myself earlier: structural homogeneity from conception to perception. Seen from the viewpoint of conception it may be that my pictures up to that point had always been coherent in logic; but only the Color Sounds are at the same time strictly developed from perception—or, as I have just said, evolve from their psychological impact on the beholder. That is the categorical difference distinguishing them from the Color Reliefs, from which the Color Sounds differ for the outsider only in nuances. (On this point, see "The Precision of Sensation," page 33.)

The Idea

The Color Sound consists of twelve steps—which is to be understood literally: each color also forms a step of the relief. From step to step the difference is extremely small; from the first to the last it is large, often complementary. What is intended is a polychrome sound of the highest homogeneity; in the experience of the beholder, the evocation of a sensation of the highest possible intensity.

The color psychologist Max Lüscher encouraged my efforts and interpreted the Intro and Extra Versions 7 and 15 (catalogs to the exhibition at Denise René/Hans Mayer, Düsseldorf, 1972 and Denise René, New York, 1973, respectively; see page 164).

Color Sound, by the way, is a concept which does not exist. I translated the German word *Farb-Klang* (color chord) literally into English, thereby emphasizing that language brings about a union of the visual and the auditory—in the sense of Baudelaire's *correspondance*.

The Realization

Typical example: Color Sound 1C, Intro and Extra Version. I wrote a detailed description of this work for the catalog to the exhibition in the Gemeinde-Galerie Emmenbrücke, 1976; see page 168.

Each Color Sound alters according to the daylight: in the cold light of morning all the warm colors become darker: in the warm light of evening it is the cold colors that darken. This change, it is true, takes place generally with all colors; in the Color Sounds it can—because of the homogeneity of the color series—be read, experienced.

The Beginnings

I designed the first Color Sounds immediately following the Color Reliefs in 1968. In the same year a serigraph was published (by Denise René/Hans Mayer, Düsseldorf/Paris), and in the following year the portfolio Color Sound 1, which was followed by two more (each with 8 serigraphs, again by Denise René/Hans Mayer). A Color Sound (No. 8) was also the object of a reproduction without an original: Walter Widmer (of the Graphische Werkstätten Basel, 1972) produced the twelve layers with masks and the colors solely by adjusting the exposure time on photographic color films.

The first presentation of the originals took place in 1972 (Galerie Denise René/Hans Mayer, Düsseldorf). The Color Sounds St. Jacques also date from this year.

The idea for Color Dome—the Mystery of Light was conceived in 1974 (as a proposal for an American museum). It was realized in 1978 at my retrospective at the Museum of Fine Arts, Solothurn.

The Color Sounds also exist as sculptures. First as Color Sound Janus, a double relief, the two faces of which have a common external color; inside they are different but complementary. A triad, each relief 350 × 350 cm in size, was first erected in the buildings of the Landesjustiz (State Department of Justice) at Siegen, 1976. The second sculpture is the Color Sound Cube, project for a spatial sculpture. In this case the internal color is the same for all four sides; externally it changes into the four primary colors.

Color Sound 7C

1968-1972
Intro Version
Nitrocellulose on phenolic resin plates
1180 × 1180 framed

Color Sounds
Homage to the Homage to the Square

Homage to Albers: arising from elective affinity, friendship, gratitude–in which what is common also implies what is different.

Albers starts with the material. He probes into color, experiments with it, is prepared to be surprised by what he finds: by the interaction. Albers is a finder.

I start with the idea. I imagine to myself the effect of the color: its specific "sound." Then I seek the tones which allow me to realize this image. I am a seeker.

Albers never mixes his colors. That is to say: he uses the color tones just as they come out of the tube. He makes up for this voluntary limitation by always having available an enormous range of all possible shades of color. Dozens of different yellows, reds, blues–and, and, and. On the back of his pictures he always notes the makes which he has used on the front.

I always mix my colors. That is to say: I use a range of only a few colors, specifically ten primary colors. This is an opportunity for a word of gratitude: I have found the pigments for my purpose with the aid of the chemist Dr. Hans Gärtner and the technician Ewald Schoohf, both of Ciba-Geigy in Basel. The criteria: the greatest purity and fastness. Using a precision balance I standardize any shade I want. And I keep the formula for each shade.

Albers starts from the phenomenon of color. I start from its effect. I am not so much interested in the stimulus of the color as in the sensation it elicits.

Color Sound 7
Intro Version, 1968/71
Nitrocellulose on phenolic resin plates
1180 × 1180 framed

Sound: high but not shrill tones. Major key. Medium volume, if anything rather soft. Flute, clarinet, piano; chirping, twittering, tremolo. Cheerful. Relaxed.

Place: sand, dunes; by the sea. In the south.

Time: spring, in the morning (or evening?).

A plenitude of sunshine; with a light, cool breeze (Extra Version). Mist through which the sun is breaking (Intro Version).

From Tokyo, Yoko Kuwasawa wrote: This picture represents for me what we call *shikisokuzeku*: the Buddhist expression for the vanity and transitoriness of all earthly existence.

(From the catalog to the exhibition at the Gallery Denise René/Hans Mayer, Düsseldorf, 1972.)

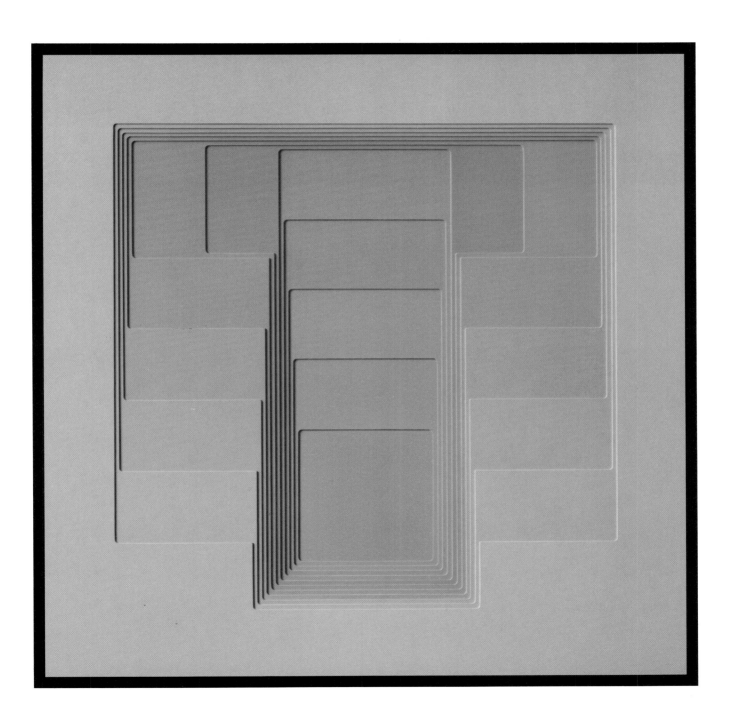

Max Lüscher:
Color Sound 15

Max Lüscher took his doctor's degree in philosophy and psychology at the university of his native city, Basel. Experimental work with the Rorschach test led him to evolve the Lüscher Color Test for the assessment of personality. This clinical test was first presented in the form it has today, to the International Congress of Psychologists at Lausanne in 1947, and this form has remained valid ever since. Since then it has been widely disseminated all over the world and has held up through numerous scientific investigations.

Karl Gerstner constructs his Color Sounds according to polarities of color and polarities of form. Between these polarities he interposes intermediate gradations which are as equal as possible in value.

In its technical perfection the construction produces emotional surprises which can be interpreted in terms of psychology. The metric regularity of the changes of color tone ("Nature"), which is measured with an electron balance, is subject to abrupt mutational leaps in its psychical expressiveness. The finely graded optical order reveals itself to be an apparent regularity. Emotional reality, on the other hand, shows that certain color tones have a highly individual antiauthoritarian quality.

To anticipate: the outer conventional appearance of relative uniformity (the even distribution of the gradations of color) demonstrates to the sensitive understanding that the separate color tones have an individuality which is immensurable and are possessed of a particular affective significance. In brief: this individuality is, like a genetic mutation, not a product which can be calculated from external (e.g., sociological) factors. This, I take it, is the intellectual message of Gerstner's Color Sound.

(From the catalog of the exhibition at Denise René, New York, 1973)

Form

Gerstner takes the square as his basic form. This is the system of order with the greatest simplicity and at the same time the highest degree of specificity because of its equal sides and its fixed right angle.

The color gradations are framed in rectangles. Gerstner fans out the frame and center, the primary, formal polarities of a picture into four polar principles of order.

He assigns to the square in the center and the square forming the frame the strongest contrasts of light and dark or hue. In this way he attains the maximum contrasting tension between the center as the focus of the picture and the frame as the surround. But at the same time the surround is the ground of the picture, its basis.

But it is the basis of the picture not only because of the color contrast, the light-dark contrast, or the inside-outside contrast, but also spatially because of the relief structure.

No frame merely imposes limits. It is always at the same time a passage, like the doorframe, the church door, the triumphal arch: a passage into another room, into another spiritual domain, into another system of values.

Gerstner documents the spiritual passage with these four dimensions.

Finally he finds a fifth possibility in inversion, by reversing the four dimensions as a whole and showing them as a mirror-inverted second picture, the verso, as it were, of the first.

Let what you will be fitted into a consistent, formal system of order, or forced into subtly balanced gradations, color itself goes its own way. It asserts its freedom, its individual independence. Its emotional significance is so out of accord with all the principles of order that it seems as if color is not subject to the laws of logic, as if chance, mutation, or indeed anarchy holds sway.

Certainly, causality according to natural laws is suspended here. What is discernible is not quantitative, metric logic but qualitative; not calculation but mathematics; not the laws of the sensory-material but the self-given laws of the mind and psyche.

Color

Anyone looking at the sequence of color shades without an understanding of color psychology sees a change from violet to green-black.

Anyone who is sensitive to the emotional content of color gradations will see that not all twelve gradations mediate twelve uniformly differing sensations. Between some color shades there are only relative differences due primarily to their different degrees of brightness. Two or three shades may display relative changes of this kind and go together as a group. In the case of other gradations, however, each is distinctly different from the one preceding or following it.

This is the surprise and the paradox of metric regularity.

In other words, there are not only an initial and a final stage but also at least five gradation ranges differing fundamentally in character, each with its entirely different emotional significance, i.e., a specific message in terms of color psychology.

The passage from one color to the next yields an entirely different view, just as a walk through the countryside produces at one turn of the path the old familiar picture while at another it reveals a totally novel scene.

View the twelve shades of the Color Sound as a whole and it is like looking down from an airplane at a richly diverse landscape. But the adventure of surprise, the emotional sidetracking and backtracking, is experienced only when the color tones are paced of. Some elicit similar, some different, and some opposite emotions.

Even so, they are quite specific emotions which are objectively alike for everyone–i.e., not subjective affects.

Once all the gradations have been traversed, the adventure lived through, what has been experienced condenses into a symbol. For one beholder it is "an interesting picture"; another gives his interpretation of the symbol: the violet corresponds to winged Eros, who through the twelve stages of darkening–from 1 to 12–congeals to death in the black.

Or he reads the picture in the reverse direction–from 12 to 1. In it he finds the resurrection and recognizes in the violet the color of those illuminated by the pentecostal spirit.

1. **Violet**

The brightest color is a blue containing a good deal of red. Violet is the oscillating combination of stimulating red with soothing blue, of fire with water. The two "elements" form hissing steam, the two colors elicit that sublimated "gaseous" emotion: fascination. Blue-violet represents sensitivity, readiness for fascination in the all-embracing original signification of Eros.

2. **Blue-violet**

The second color gradation is a violet that contains more of soothing blue and less of stimulating red.

In other respects, however, the effect is akin to that of the first gradation.

3. **Violet-blue**

The third color gradation becomes calmer still. The flickering and oscillation between blue and red disappears in favor of pacification in blue.

In other respects, however, the effect is akin to the second gradation.

4. **Red-blue**

In itself the fourth gradation seems to be simply blue. But because the blue which soothes and stabilizes the emotions has been mixed with a trace of red, it begins to vibrate. Blue, which mediates cool tranquillity, harmonious content, and intellectual clarity, is heightened through the red element to readiness for enthusiasm, for the intensity of enveloping spirituality, which expresses itself as religion and philosophy.

5. **Pure blue**

In the step from the fourth to the fifth gradation impulsive red, activity, has vanished completely. Pure blue mediates calm, content divested of emotion. It is opposed to green, which means stillness.

Through its tranquillity and its unalloyed unambiguity blue is marked by clarity of effect. This "clear calm" corresponds to quiet self-confidence, to the integrated sense of self, to wisdom.

States and moods are described as "blue" if they are freed from all sense of purposive striving.

6. **Green-blue**

If only a little green is added to quiet blue, peaceful contentment becomes cool stillness. Self-confidence grows into pride, inward integration becomes outward aloofness: cool reserve.

7. **Blue-green**

Between the sixth and seventh gradation green increases so much that optically the color is between blue and green.

The meaning also changes continuously and culminates in the next gradation.

8. **Blue-green**

The more green added to blue, the colder and harder the effect produced by the color. Self-confidence becomes arrogant pride, narrow-minded crankiness, willful obstinacy. In blue-green we find expressed the stubbornness, the *idios cosmos* of the idiot (literally: *idios* = own; *cosmos* = world, system). This color, heightened to its one-track climax, becomes a sign of schizophrenia if, at the same time, equal liking is shown for the next gradation, the completely different, sensual-soft, animal-warm brown-green.

9. **Brown-green**

If hard, cold blue-green is mixed with brown, its meaning switches to the opposite pole. Hard, cool wilfulness crumbles, and with brown-green a sensual animal well-being emerges. The warmth of the stable and the security of the nest, an unproblematic vegetative existence and feral primitiveness, are betokened.

10. **Green-brown**

From the ninth to the tenth gradation the green becomes so dark that it turns into a distinct brown tone. As the bright colors fade, their power to stimulate peters out.

11. **Green-brown**

Green vanishes. Brown approaches black. Passivity and the extinction of stimulation ensue. If gradation 10 is still felt to be pleasant, comfortable and peaceful, then life is expiring. Peace is changing into death.

12. **Green-black**

In the last and twelfth gradation darkness gains the upper hand. The activity of the light is snuffed out. Nothingness dominates.

The animal green-brown of the tenth gradation, the vegetative life, peters out in black, the color of denial, of final resignation. The violet Eros congeals in black death.

(From the catalog of the exhibition at Denise René, New York, 1973)

Color Sound 15

1968-1972, 1973
Intro Version
Nitrocellulose on phenolic resin plates
1180 × 1180 framed

167

Color Sound 1C

Extra Version, 1968/1972
(Intro Version on page 170)
Nitrocellulose on phenolic resin plates
1180 × 1180 framed
Branco Weiss collection, Zurich

Color Sound: Color to hear. Sound to see.

* * *

The phrase "Color Sound" is my literal translation of the German *Farb-Klang*. I wanted to show that here language unites "color"–from the domain of the visual–with "sound"–from the domain of the auditory.

German has a number of other such combinations: *Klang-Farbe* (timbre) or *Farb-Ton* (color chord), for example. A deep note is said to be "dark"; a high note is said to be "bright." Language teaches me to see tones–and vice versa.

A color is "loud" (orange), or "soft" (very light blue). Or "shrill" (magenta) or "dull" (brown-gray).

Not only can I see colors, I can also feel them: Red as "warm," blue as "cold" (the blue and red faucets). Or taste: pink is "sweet," olive is "tart." And so forth.

* * *

In his poem "Correspondances" Baudelaire writes about the most intimate relationship between "perfumes, colors, and sounds." As the universe is a living unit, it follows of necessity that the perceptible forms in all their profusion are actually the echo of a single reality.

* * *

Each Color Sound consists of twelve color tones. The difference from one color tone to the next is small: from the first to the last it is–in three dimensions–relatively large: from the nuance to the complement, from light to dark, from pure to impure.

* * *

Each Color Sound originates in the idea of a union of sound and color. In moments of euphoria the result might be seen–or heard–as the music of the spheres in the cosmos of the colors.

* * *

Considered analytically, each Color Sound represents a certain configuration in this cosmos. All twelve color tones lie like points in more or less close proximity at regular intervals along a line–or, more precisely, a specific spatial curve.

Color Sound 1 is the cipher for the idea: a warm, pure vermilion becomes colder, impurer and darker until it reaches a natural anthracite–or vice versa.

Vermilion, the most active and stimulating of all colors, is the dominant in Color Sound 1C. Starting with vermilion, the color tones change to carmine, scarlet, purple, magenta, violet–gradually merging into blue: the psychological countercolor of red.

However, the blue is not visible here. It is masked by another transformation: that from the highest possible purity (of the vermilion) to being com-

Color Sound 1C

1968-1972, 1973, Intro Version
Nitrocellulose on phenolic resin plates
1180 × 1180 framed

pletely grayed down. That is, the colors do not change their tone alone but also become increasingly grayed; and where blue should be, there is anthracite, a dark, neutral gray.

Dark gray: related to blue and to black in character, passive like them. If blue is absorption and black is death, dark gray remains indifferent; compared with black it contains a little hope; compared with blue it is duller and more impersonal.

* * *

All in all: opposites, merging into each other, one after the other or at the same time, in tiny gradations, imperceptibly, so to speak. Not only as a visual experience but also (and above all) as a state of psychological suspension, a balance of different vibrations.

* * *

The "C" in the title means that there are versions A, B and C of this idea, each being the heightening of the one preceding it. In the case of version B new experiences led to an improvement of A. In the case of C new pigments allowed the original idea to be realized with more precision.

"Extra Version" means that the dominant vermilion is outside, spreads, comes toward the beholder. As distinct from "Intro Version": here the vermilion is inside, holds back, and waits for the beholder to go toward it.

* * *

The colors of Color Sound 1C are adjusted for neutral midday light at about 7500 degrees Kelvin.

That is to say: In the morning light, when the color temperature is lower, the red looks as dark as the gray. And the middle magenta tones glow in purity. In the evening light, when the color temperature is higher, the warm red tones are bright and radiant. And the magenta tones are hardly to be distinguished from the dark violet and gray tones.

* * *

The Color Sounds do not consist solely of a series of continuously changing colors; they also change continuously as a whole. They are echoes of the sun, echoes to be seen.

(From the catalog for the exhibition in the Gemeinde-Galerie Emmenbrücke, Lucerne, 1976)

Color Sound 8

1968-1972, 1973, Extra Version
Nitrocellulose on phenolic resin plates
1180 × 1180 framed

Color Sound 49

1968-1972, 1973, Extra Version
Nitrocellulose on phenolic resin plates
1180 × 1180 framed

173

Color Sound 4D

1968-1972, 1973, Extra Version
Nitrocellulose on phenolic resin plates
1180 × 1180 framed

174

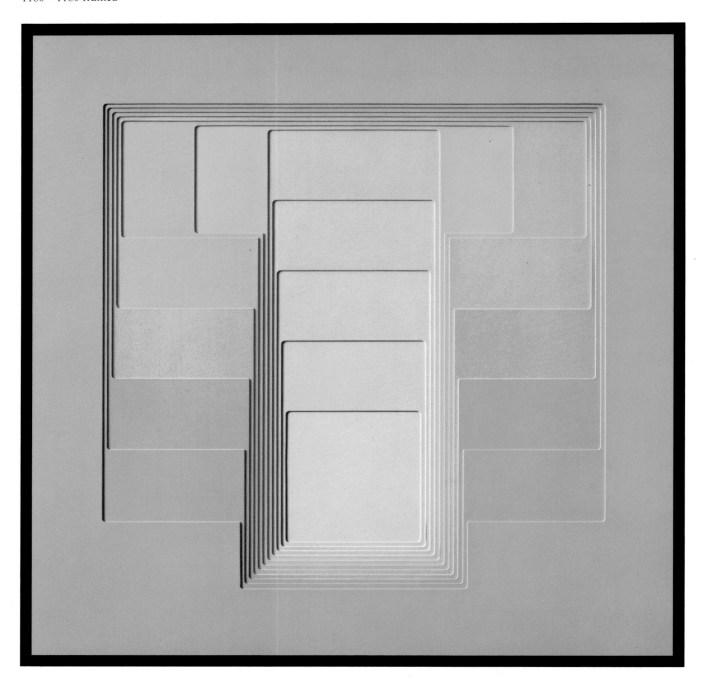

Color Sound 2A

1968-1972, 1973, Intro Version
Nitrocellulose on phenolic resin plates, 596 × 596 framed
Jean Rueff collection, Basel

Color Dome

1974-1978
Acrylic lacquers on polyester
Twelve-part cycle from the Color Sounds
Each 1700 × 1700
Installation, Museum of Fine Arts, Solothurn

Color Sound St. Jacques 6

1972-1973
Intro Version
Nitrocellulose on phenolic resin plates
596 × 596

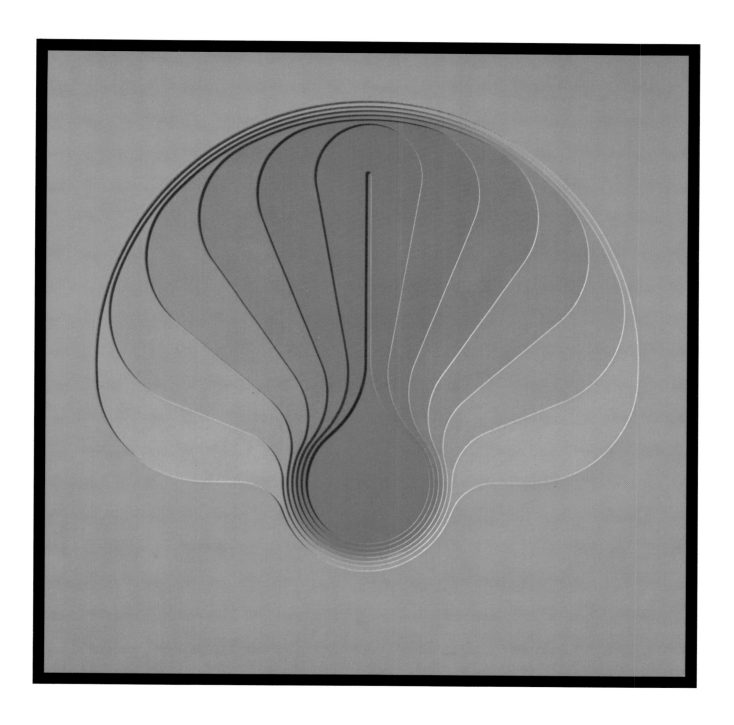

8. The Color Forms

The Starting Point

I based all the Color Sounds on the same formal structure so as to be able to concentrate on the color. In the Color Forms I wanted to include form as well. Not as I had done in the formal predecessors to the Color Sounds, the Color Reliefs–out of sheer pleasure in combinatory operations–but in the way I explored color in the Color Sounds: according to their psychological expression.

A horizontal is as different from a vertical as white is from black, cold from warm, passivity from activity, death from life–as Kandinsky says. To him we are also indebted for a correlation of color and form. According to him blue goes with the circle, yellow with the triangle, and red with the square.

I had two questions. First, whether I could accept Kandinsky's hypotheses; and second, whether I could develop a system out of them. That is to say, to merge forms continuously into each other in the way I had done with colors.

The Idea

Answer to the first question: in principle, yes. I found that many of Kandinsky's hypotheses had been confirmed by numerous authors in the literature. For example: that the correlation of blue and the circle is, so to speak, undisputed. In other respects, however, I did not want to correlate basic geometric forms with physical primary colors; I was interested exclusively in the psychical/psychological aspect. Therefore, for me, yellow does not correlate with the triangle but with a star-shaped figure which–in my view–expresses the radiance of the color better than the triangle. I also see red as being square but I stand the square on its corner so as to express the main characteristic of red–the ambivalence of dynamism and strength. In distinction to Kandinsky I likewise regard green as a color with primary autonomy. Its form is that of sine curves round the straight lines of the square and–in spite of the strict construction–gives expression to the vegetative and quiet spirit. See "The Color-Form Continuum," page 184.

Answer to the second question: yes, these four basic forms could be made into a system, by being arranged to fit into one another in the order of the natural color sequence with as many intermediate steps as desired to provide gradation. In any case systematization already exists inasmuch as the complementary colors yellow and blue and red and green each make a complementary pair of forms.

The Realization

Before I could execute these pictures I had to find the answer to an economic problem: how was the vast amount of work entailed by the construction of the intermediate stages to be handled? At a fairly early stage I wanted to use the computer, but some years were to pass before I found in Klaus Thomas the ideal programmer and partner. The result was a series of eight computer drawings: four Con-Versions and four Di-Versions from the primary colors (see page 205).

It would have been consistent with the idea also to produce the colors–or at least to have them calculated–by computer, but so far there is no instrumentarium which is more precise than sensation.

The Color Forms are executed as reliefs, like the Color Sounds.

The Beginnings

I can no longer give an exact date for the idea. However, it is considerably older than that of the Color Sounds, which were executed earlier. From time to time I tried things out, like this effort with the octagon corresponding to violet:

In between I executed the pair of pictures Color Ring/Color Cross (1968); again a kind of Color Form. They represent–but in color and form–a pair of opposites of primal symbolic significance. Color Cross: expansive, radiating outward, active; Color Ring: conservative, radiating inward, passive.

In 1969 I had my first opportunity, at the Massachusetts Institute of Technology to follow the results on the computer screen. Collaboration with Klaus Thomas began in 1970 and continued for some years. The computer drawings have been finished since 1975; the color drafts since 1976. The final version was completed in 1979. *Final* means that the first definitive version is ready. Others will follow, particularly those in which the color does *not* correlate with the form, thereby expressing an intended state of tension.

181

Color Cross Archetype

1968/1976
Nitrocellulose on phenolic resin plates
1180 × 1180 framed

Color Ring Archetype

1968/1976
Nitrocellulose on phenolic resin plates
1180 × 1180 framed

The Color-Form Continuum

(The Precision of Sensation, 4)

Wilhelm Ostwald (in *Mathetische Farbenlehre*): We must first ascertain whether we see anything else besides colors. The answer usually comes promptly: it is to the effect that besides colors, we also see forms. With an implicit tendency to regard these as what is seen first and most generally.

However, a more searching investigation shows at once that colors are in fact the first and most general item in what is seen. If we look at the content of our visual field absolutely directly without concerning ourselves with the "meaning" of this content, i.e., what thoughts, associations and memories it elicits, it presents itself as a diversity of colored patches spread over a surface.

Do we see colors or forms?
Or colors and forms?

These patches sometimes merge continuously into each other and consequently differ in color from one place to another without it being possible to say exactly where one color starts and another finishes. But in the majority of cases the patches border on each other without merging, so that boundary lines are formed between them. It is only out of the combined effect of such color patches that what we call form emerges; hence form is a result of the presence of color and its spatial arrangement.

Colors are the elements of what is seen.

* * *

Ostwald, philosopher of the energic imperative, thus turned upside down the Cartesian world view in which color is almost a textbook example of a secondary quality whereas form is posited as a primary quality.

Is color a secondary and form a primary quality?

Descartes, the philosopher of the rational imperative, took as his starting point the old doubt in the reliability of the senses and turned doubt into a method, and with it reached the fixed point of *cogito ergo sum*–and from there attained the conviction that everything is true that we cognize *clare et distincte*. However, all that we cognize *clare et distincte* in Nature is the mathematical, but this is subject to geometry, i.e., form.

* * *

Whether color has primacy over form; whether form has primacy over color: this question–curiously enough–has exercised the best minds over the centuries.

Kant (in the *Critique of Judgment*, "Analysis of the Beautiful"): In painting, sculpture, indeed in all the pictorial arts, in architecture and landscape gardening, insofar as they are fine arts, the important thing is drawing, in which it is not what gives pleasure to the senses but what gratifies through its form that makes the basis for taste. The colors which illuminate the outline are part of the charm; but while they render the object in itself more lively to the senses they cannot make it beautiful and worthy of contemplation.

* * *

Heinrich Meyer (in *Hypothetical History of Color*, a contribution to Goethe's *Theory of Colors*): According to Pliny's statement all the old traditions are agreed that painting actually began with the outline of a human shadow; and this may be accepted as probable on the condition that we do not think of real shadows or outline figures but rather of experiments with line in which an attempt is made to draw a form on a flat surface, for, after all, this is really the basis of painting.

* * *

In art the dispute over the primacy of color or form started an academic war. In the seventeenth century the adherents of Poussin–the Poussinists–argued for form; the adherents of Rubens–the Rubenists–for color.

Or is form a secondary and color a primary quality?

On visiting the Dresden gallery, Schiller found that the big paintings of Rubens would without doubt have been works of art if they had been painted without colors.

"I cannot rid myself of the thought that the colors convey something untruthful to me, because they seem to be differently colored depending on whether the light falls this way or that or on the viewpoint from which I see them this way or that. The pure outline would give me a much truer picture."

* * *

Thank heavens there was no losing side in this war. How much poorer the world would be today if a contrite Rubens had retired into himself, or if the principles of Poussin had not only been adopted literally but–what would have been still worse–in opposition to Poussin himself.

In Goethe–typically–we have two spirits in one breast. The classicist cherished the ideal of the line, the form; the romantic was inclined to color.

* * *

Goethe the classicist was influenced by Winckelmann, who took classical sculpture as his starting point (believing it–erroneously–to be colorless). For him lines of incomparable beauty were expressed in forms; he wanted to exclude color as far as he could and assign it only a secondary status.

Or is the dispute about the primacy of color and form a dispute for its own sake?

Goethe the romantic may have been influenced by Diderot, whose *Essay on Painting* he translated into German (in *Schriften zur Kunst*).

Diderot: "Drawing gives things their form; color gives them life, it is the divine breath which animates everything." Further: "All representation of form without color is symbolic. Color alone makes the work of art true, brings it close to reality."

* * *

The quarrel over primacy is particularly curious in view of the fact that the protagonists were relatively well informed on the nature of form but knew little about the nature of light.

Hegel (in the *Lectures on Aesthetics*): "Drawing... can be reduced to general laws less readily than perspective. And color even less still. The color sense must be an artistic characteristic, a specific way of seeing and conceiving color tones which exist and also an important aspect of the reproductive imagination and invention."

Diderot (in *Essay on Painting*) on the same theme: "In the case of drawing we have... if not a complete theory at least certain principles; certain rules and measures which can be handed on. In the case of color, on the other hand, there is neither theory nor principles, or anything else, that can be handed on... It is a phenomenon which appeals only to the feeling; and can thus be produced only through feeling and, as it were, instinctively."

It was to remedy precisely this deficiency that Goethe wrote his *Theory of Colors* (see page 42).

Might it not be that colors were assigned secondary status because little was known about them?

Even down to the present day investigation into the essential nature of color comes up against serious obstacles. There is no homogeneous interdisciplinary knowledge, and knowledge even in the specialist areas–mathematics, physics, chemistry, physiology, psychology–consists largely of insights into the gaps that remain to be closed.

One thing is certain: our knowledge about color is still deficient.

* * *

One basic difficulty is of a material nature: so far it is quite impossible to produce all possible colors chemically. True, we know in what ranges of the physical spectrum there are color tones–particularly in the ranges of magenta, violet, and blue–which are considerably purer than the known hues. But generations of color chemists all over the world have not yet succeeded in finding the pigments for them.

* * *

Newton can claim the glory of having been the first to shed light in the obscurity of speculations. However, it was not until the nineteenth century that men awoke to the need of remedying the lack of rational knowledge not only in physics but in all branches of knowledge.

Yet it was an artist–Philipp Otto Runge, and a romantic to boot–who was the first to order the totality of colors in a systematic manner: in his spherical model, in which the black-white poles form an axis and the colors the equator.

* * *

Even during Goethe's lifetime Schopenhauer philosophized "On Seeing and the Colors." His aim: to supply the theory for Goethe's *Theory of Colors* (he failed).

Physicists, physiologists, and psychologists gave knowledge a fillip. Young formulated the three-color theory; Weber, the founder of psychophysics, and later Fechner sought a system of physical measurement for psychic sensation. Wundt founded experimental psychology. Hering and Helmholtz improved our knowledge of vision.

In mid-century the chemists Hofmann and Perkin discovered the aniline dyes of unprecedented brilliance (the Impressionists were greatly taken by them; unfortunately the colors turned out to be nowhere near so stable as they were brilliant).

* * *

Of the many others whose names might be entered in the list, I will pick out two outsiders: Humbert de Superville and Charles Henry.

The artistic all-rounder Humbert de Superville (artist, author, essayist) published in 1827 *Sur les signes inconditionnels dans l'art*, including a table "on the basic fact of the unconditional and identical value of linear and colored signs."

Under the influence of Lavater, Superville took the physiognomy of the human face as his starting point. He observed that the face acquires a cheerful expression if the axis of the eyes from the root of the nose is directed upward; a doleful expression if it is directed downward; and an expression of equanimity if it is horizontal.

From this Superville deduced rules of general validity: nose = vertical line; eyes = straight line in the three directions just described. The vertical is correlated with black; the horizontal with white, the upward-inclined diagonal with red, the downward-inclined one with blue.

* * *

The intellectual all-rounder Charles Henry (chemist, physicist, physiologist) gave a scientific basis to Superville's hypotheses and developed them further.

According to Henry the upward-pointing direction also corresponds to joy; the downward-pointing one to sorrow. To this pair of opposites he added another: movement from left to right tends toward the pleasant; from right to left toward the unpleasant.

These elementary, linear movements "from below upward" and "from left to right" again correspond to the elementary colors red, orange, and yellow. "From above downward" and "from right to left" to green, blue, and violet.

* * *

Henry went a step further still and evolved a–to his mind–logical model in the form of a circular area. On its vertical axis were located–from north to south, as it were–red-green; and on its horizontal axis–from west to east–violet-yellow. In the upper quadrant on the right–from north to east–were located the cheerful

Colors and forms are complementary to each other.

colors; in the lower quadrant on the left–from south to west–the sad ones.

In between it was possible to have any number of gradations which could be calculated with the aid of a *rapporteur esthétique*–according to Gaussian number sequences.

* * *

Henry sought a rational way of arriving at combinations which are congruent psychically and aesthetically. While I can understand the intention, I cannot share the conclusions. To me it looks as if Henry had put the wrong finger on the right spot, which was nevertheless an achievement that earned him the interest of his Post-impressionist contemporaries. Seurat and Signac, as has been shown, made good use of it.

* * *

What I value in Henry, reservations aside, is that he was not concerned with a dispute over primacy but with insight, with discovery, which as such can only be value-free.

Perhaps the reason why color was assigned a secondary status was not that too little was known about it, but because in Descartes' time the mathematics descriptive of Nature was restricted to geometry. At least this deficiency has been made good today.

Von Weizsäcker: Modern mathematics has advanced far beyond this view. We can even describe non-visualizable facts mathematically by means of abstract algebra; and every attempt to organize the continuum of color qualities structurally comes under the heading of structural research in modern mathematics.

* * *

As I see it, color and form are two categories which not only supplement but also condition each other reciprocally. There is no form without color, no color without form. But any form can be imagined in any color–and vice versa.

Colors and forms determine each other.

Each category has its own unmistakable peculiarities but the categories are in conformity with one another.

Colors and forms correspond to each other.

* * *

In principle there are two different types of correlation between color and form. They may be illustrated by reference to cartography: we distinguish between topological and typological maps; the first being concerned with the place, and the second with the type.

* * *

A political map, for example, is topological. In this case the cartographic units–Switzerland, Italy, France, i.e., countries–are distinguished by arbitrarily chosen colors: yellow for Switzerland, red for Italy, blue for France. That is to say that color here is used as a distinguishing feature; the fact that Switzerland is yellow has no significance. The main thing is that its color is different from that of Italy, and Italy has a different color from Switzerland and France because the three countries are contiguous–and so forth.

(The problem, incidentally, is known in the topological division of modern mathematics as the four-color problem. That is, four colors–not more–are necessary to distinguish between any number of places standing in any relation to each other).

Topological correspondence: color and form represent two independent systems. The opposite is typological correspondence: form and color are congruent, they build an integrated system.

Topological correspondence
Typological correspondence

An example: tectonic maps, say, of differences in altitude on the earth's surface. The distance between the highest and the lowest point is divided into units; each unit corresponds to a color on a graded scale: from white (8000 meters above) to dark blue (8000 meters below sea level).

190

A Gothic stained-glass window is topological. A linear drawing (further emphasized by the lead cames) is colored: the noncongruence is due to the spirituality of what is portrayed. A picture by Titian is typological. Titian draws with color; the congruence is due to the naturalism of what is portrayed.

In the case of Mondrian a typological period can be discerned: the early pictures, which were painted in terms of color; and a topological: the later works, which were conceived in terms of line. In the case of Lohse it is the other way round: in early pictures he marked a formally logical structure with arbitrarily selected colors; in the later pictures the structure is the result of making color the binding element in the picture.

* * *

Heinrich Meyer errs, by the way, if he assumes (like Pliny) that visual art originated from line. From the very outset there have been cave paintings (those of Altamira, for example) which were originally conceived in terms of color. But this–again–could have been known to neither of them.

* * *

Topological–typological: by making this distinction in principle I do not wish to argue in favor of any principle. This again is a statement of principle to be remembered if, in what follows, I concern myself exclusively with the typological correspondence between color and form.

* * *

It is fruitful to start with Kandinsky. With his two publications *Concerning the Spiritual in Art* (1912) and *Point and Line to Plane* (1926).

Kandinsky begins his argument with the horizontal: "In the human mind this corresponds to the line... on which man stands and moves. The horizontal is therefore a cold, weight-bearing base."

The correspondence of colors and lines

Entirely opposed to this line externally and internally and perpendicular to it we have the vertical, in which flatness is replaced by height, and therefore cold by warmth.

The third typical kind of straight line is the diagonal, which deviates from the two aforementioned lines at the same angle and thus has the same inclination to both of them, which determines its inner sonority–the harmonious union of cold and warmth. And a greater internal tension.

* * *

The color corresponding to the horizontal is black, and to the vertical white. Both are "silent colors," just as the straight lines mentioned are "silent lines"; black the symbol of death, white the symbol of birth.

Logically Kandinsky correlates the diagonal with gray; but also with red–adding the comment: "The parallelism diagonal-red is stated here as a proposition, for which the detailed proofs would go far beyond the theme of this book. To put it briefly: red is distinguished from yellow and blue by its characteristic property of lying on the plane [there will be more on this subject], from black and white by its intense inner ebullition, its inherent tension."

Lines of indeterminate position–i.e., neither horizontal, nor vertical, nor diagonal–correspond to yellow and blue; or, to be more precise, if we include Kandinsky's correlation of colors and angles, yellow corresponds to the acute, blue to the obtuse, and red to the right angle.

From lines and angles Kandinsky comes to the plane, to form in the narrower sense.

The correspondence of colors and planes

Kandinsky: "Form in the narrower sense is in any case nothing more than the demarcation of one plane from another. That is its characterization as regards externals. But just as every external also necessarily contains within itself an internal (which is apparent in differing degrees), so every form also has an inner content. Form is therefore the externalization of the inner content... Even if it is quite abstract and resembles a geometrical form it still has its inner sonority, it is a spiritual being with attributes which are identical with this form."

* * *

Colors and forms
have their specific expressions.

Like form, color also has its inner sonority. Both are means of exercising a direct influence on the spirit. Kandinsky: "They are both keys. The eye is the hammer. The spirit is the piano with many strings. The artist is the hand which, through this or that key, sets the human spirit vibrating appropriately."

The effect which colors and forms exert on each other is inevitable, with some colors being accentuated in their value by some forms and dulled by others.

Kandinsky: "A triangle filled with yellow, a circle with blue, a square with green, and again a triangle with green, a circle with yellow, a square with blue, and so forth. These are all entirely dissimilar entities and produce entirely different effects."

* * *

The question now is this: the expression of what color corresponds to the expression of what form?

In my search for an answer, I start with the colors yellow and blue–following Goethe, who in turn followed the alchemists, in whose philosophy this opposed pair formed the oldest representatives of color; blue–as the darkest of the pure colors–darkness, yellow–as the brightest–the offspring of light.

* * *

Rudolf Steiner: "Yellow must be radiant. Yellow must spread; in the middle it is saturated, towards the outside it becomes steadily weaker. Blue, through its inner essence, demands the exact opposite of yellow. That is to say, it radiates from outside inward. It is most saturated at the margin and least in the interior."

Yellow radiates outward, blue radiates inward.

According to Steiner, both yellow and blue can be represented as a point, or, more specifically, as a circular area. In the yellow circle the center is usually saturated, the periphery least; the color fades away into the background. In the blue circle it is the other way round: the periphery is most saturated; toward the center the saturation diminishes.

* * *

Kandinsky correlates the circle with blue, and the triangle with yellow (he does not make Steiner's distinction as regards color saturation).

It is natural enough to correlate blue with the circle. Blue and the circle are *per se* restful, passive, timeless.

In the Lüscher Test blue means satisfaction, security–qualities which can be readily ascribed to the attributes of the circle.

* * *

In the case of yellow, matters are less clear-cut. But the difference between the ideas of Kandinsky and Steiner is not unbridgeable.

Steiner's demand that yellow must be radiant is, after all, also fulfilled by the triangle. The acute angles of its form point beyond its plane, they radiate. This effect is further intensified if we imagine the triangle to be expanded into a star. And if we imagine a star with an infinity of beams, we then have Steiner's version: a circle saturated in the center and fading outward into the background.

It is, incidentally, curious that no one has ever seen a star in the form in which it has been represented from time immemorial. In this case the correspondence between color and form is evident.

* * *

In the Lüscher Test yellow means expansion, unfolding–again qualities which are not irreconcilable with the properties of the triangle.

* * *

It is entirely warrantable to see the triangle/circle as corresponding complementary forms to the complementary colors yellow/blue: the first consists of a minimum number of angles (three angles define the plane absolutely); the second consists of a maximum number of angles (that is, infinitely many).

The complementary pair to yellow/blue is formed by red/green, which proceeds as a combination out of the first: red as higher (as heightening), green as lower (as flattening). Question: which is the corresponding complementary pair in terms of form?

* * *

Blue
corresponds to the circle.

Yellow
corresponds to the star.

193

Kandinsky hits on a startling suggestion. He correlates both red and green with the square. Green in *Concerning the Spiritual in Art*, red in *Point and Line to Plane*. The contradiction is resolved by the reasons he gives: both colors have a characteristic in common, namely, they are colors of transition; both lie–on different sides of the color circle–between yellow and blue.

* * *

Red is also a color of transition for Steiner, an equalization of yellow and blue. He writes: "It will neither radiate nor become incrusted nor dam itself up. It remains in calm redness, it will not volatilize, it asserts itself."

This statement by Steiner squares with that of Kandinsky: that red lies on the plane (see above) whereas yellow comes toward one and blue flees away. This property of lying-firm-on-the-plane corresponds to the form of the square: it moves neither forward nor backward, neither to the right nor to the left, neither upward nor downward.

Red
corresponds to the square.

* * *

Red-square is a provisional guide. But green-square? In spite of the common characteristic red and green are not identical; far from it. Like yellow and blue they differ and are complementary to each other. And that is what the form must also express; it must be complementary to the square.

Steiner has nothing to say on this point either. For him green belongs to a category which is different from red/yellow/blue (it represents "the dead picture of life").

Is green a primary color?

This uncertainty brings to light a controversial question which also has a long tradition behind it: whether green is to be assigned the status of a primary color or not.

* * *

Mondrian banished this color not only from his thinking but also from his mind. Once, when visiting Kandinsky, he changed places with him and sat with his back to the window so that he did not have to look at the green of the trees.

* * *

Newton distinguished seven colors in the spectrum which in their relations to each other corresponded to the seven intervals of the scale. Schopenhauer was surprised at this: "He [Newton] had only to open his eyes to see that in the prismatic spectrum there are not seven colors at all but only four, of which... the two middle ones, blue and yellow, overlap and thus form green."

194

I am surprised at Schopenhauer: why should he assume that in the physical spectrum two different regions of wavelength should mix–as opposed to the others?

I feel like Carl Friedrich von Weizsäcker, who admits: "I could never quite understand with my naive experience of colors why green appears here [in Goethe's *Theory of Colors*] as merely a compound color of blue and yellow, just as if the material possibility well known to the painter of producing green by mixing its neighboring colors in the spectrum were a reason for denying this color phenomenal originality."

* * *

Kandinsky was concerned with the correlation between geometric forms and primary colors. This being granted, his correlations can also be reproduced. But is it correct to proceed from given primary colors or basic forms?

With regard to color it has not yet been possible to fix a norm. And even in the case of the undisputed primary colors yellow/red/blue it remains undecided which yellow, which red, and which blue satisfy the quality of the primary color.

And with regard to forms the case is anything but unequivocal. True, there are the platonic figures which are defined by the same length of side. The triangle is quite definitely a basic form with sides of the same length and equal angles. The same goes for the square. And the pentagon. But what about polygons having 17, 18, 19, and so on sides? Is there any dividing line between polygons which are basic forms and those which are basic forms no longer?

Or do polygons with an increasing number of sides diminish in quality as a basic form?–Right up to the preeminent case of the circle, which has an infinite number of corners, that is to say none at all?

* * *

I am concerned in my speculations neither with physically defined primary colors nor with basic geometric forms–even if there were norms for them. I am interested solely in colors and forms which are elementary in respect of the sensation they evoke.

For this reason I have started with the colors of the psychologist, specifically, of the Lüscher Color Test. And I have determined the forms according to criteria which remain to be discussed.

What are primary colors?

What are basic forms?

195

My intention: to design a model in which the correspondence between elementary colors and elementary forms (elementary as just defined) contains the sum of all that I could learn and have myself experienced: the color-form continuum.

The color-form continuum is a sensory model.

* * *

Here again the starting point: the color pair blue/yellow. In this connection I start from the correspondence blue-circle as self-evident (Figure 1, page 197).

What must the counterform–determined psychologically, not geometrically–for yellow look like?

Logically it must have a concave form instead of the convex form of the circle. I produce this by placing a horizontal and a vertical axis through the circular area and folding the quadrants inward. In this way I obtain a four-rayed star, a cruciform star, the acute angles of which, so to speak, contain *in extremis* the acute angles of the triangle (Figure 2, page 197).

* * *

The forms which are correlated with the color pair red/green have one more condition to fulfil. They must not only stand in a complementary relation to each other (in their fashion); they must also be inscribable between the two extremes convex/concave-yellow/blue.

* * *

Again I take one of Kandinsky's correspondences as my starting point: red-square. The square expresses–like red–clarity, strength, definiteness.

But Kandinsky correlates not only the square but also the diagonal with red. Reason: the diagonal, unlike free oblique straight lines, rests firmly on the plane, and unlike horizontals and verticals, has a high inner tension.

In respect of the square the stress is on strength; in respect of the diagonal on tension–an ambivalence which is characteristic of red. For this reason I have united the square and diagonal by standing the square on its corner, changing its function to that of the diagon.

The diagon lies precisely between the blue form of the circle and the yellow form of the star. In this way the basic elements of the red side of the color-form continuum are given (Figure 3, page 197).

* * *

Now for the green side. What must the form be like which stands in a complementary relation to the red diagon, which can be inscribed between the blue/yellow forms–and, needless to say, corresponds to green?

196

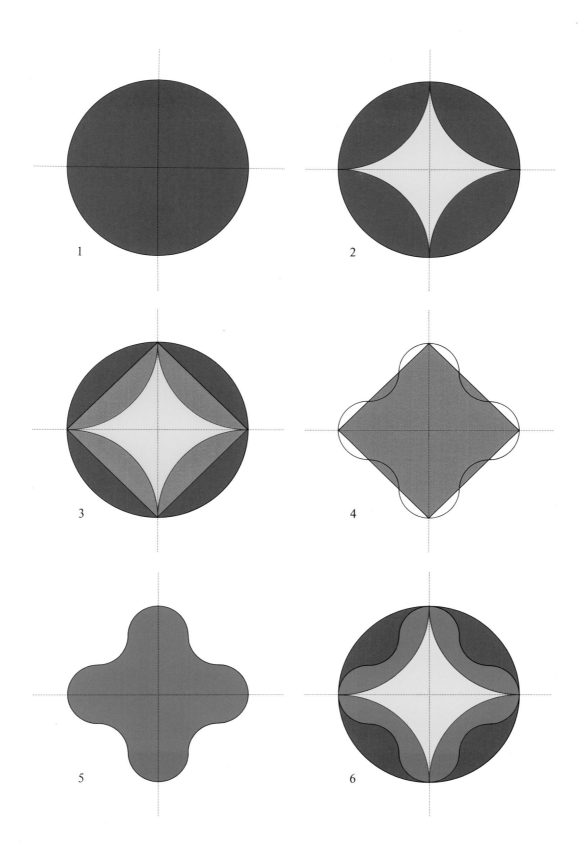

7

Color Form

Archetypal Conversion Cycle, 1970-1975, 1977
Nitrocellulose on phenolic resin plates, 800 × 800 unframed
Paul Gredinger collection, Düsseldorf

201

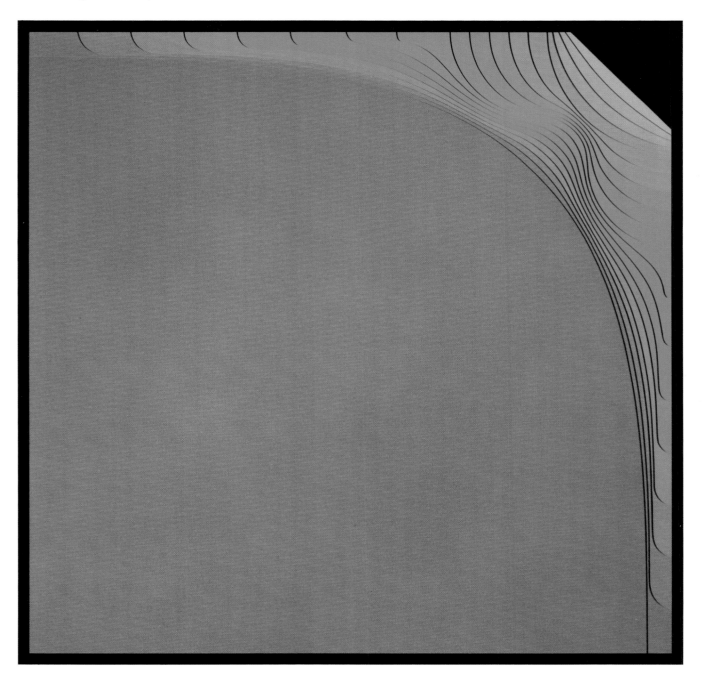

8

The characteristic of the square is its four right angles and the straight lines of its sides of equal length. I obtain a complementary form if I dissolve both the right angles and the straight lines: the straight lines of the square become sine curves which pass through the right angles of the corners as arcs (Figure 4, page 197). A new integral figure emerges which, while deriving from the diagon, is itself no longer diagonal but oriented vertically/horizontally: a kind of cloverleaf, which I call the sinuon because of its construction (Figure 5, page 197).

The sinuon is both a counterform of the red diagon and inscribable between the blue circle and yellow star–and corresponds to the color green, for which it stands.

Whereas the square placed on its corner is hard-edged, crystalline/inorganic, the form for green is fluent, vegetable/organic.

* * *

Hans Werthmüller (in *The World Process and the Colors*): Green = *bios*, vegetable kingdom, we, mother; red = psyche, animal kingdom, I, father.

In the Lüscher Test green means will, self-assertion; red means drive, impact.

Thus the basic elements of the green side of the color-form continuum are also given (Figure 6, page 197).

* * *

In the next stage these basic elements are to be extended to the intended continuum in which the color forms merge into each other at regular intervals–forming a unit without beginning or end.

That colors form a continuum *per se* is a known fact: it is their nature. Any color can be turned by a series of continuous steps into any other. But what about forms? Here I cannot refer to a generally valid model like the color solid, but I can illustrate the principles of transformation by an example: starting with a small black sphere–the egg–the tadpole turns by imperceptibly small steps into a big green frog.

If the frog is taken to be not a form that has grown in accordance with the genetic code but a given form, it follows that basically different forms like two basically different colors can be merged continuously into each other. Further, as the egg and frog stand for any forms, they can also be replaced by any forms. Condition: the transformation takes place on the time axis.

By analogy with what has been said above, it is no problem to realize the color-form continuum as, say, a

The basic forms of the continuum are called Circle, Cruciform Star, Diagon, Sinuon.

199

The color continuum is known.

The form continuum is still to be discovered.

film: one basic element–yellow for example–would be transformed by small steps of any size into the next–red for example; from there to blue to green to yellow and so forth.

But what interested me more was to know how to represent the continuum on the spatial axis. As a simultaneous event, as a picture?

* * *

The program (to be understood in both senses of the word, for the program presented could be realized only through a computer program) consisted in combining the basic forms of circle, diagon, star, and sinuon with each other round a common center. In such a way that each–and any intermediate form–returns to itself after all the other forms have been run through, in the form of a cyclic permutation.

The result is the emergence of a continuum of a specific color form which–from outside inward or vice versa–runs through all the other color forms and returns to itself. Figure 7, page 198, shows the continuum from blue to blue; Figure 8, page 200, the continuum from red to red. In which connection it should be added that not only the elementary color forms but also each intermediate stage can be the first and final station.

The pictures of the color-form continuum show one of its aspects at a time.

In the course of the work I have found that color-form correspondences can be expressed in pictures which, first, consist of only one quarter of the original figuration and, second, are not closed. These structures, reduced to the essentials, are shown in Figures 9-12 on page 205.

Figures 13-16 show the same quarters, as it were in a different direction. This calls for comment.

In the color form in Figure 9 the mutation proceeds–from inside outward–from yellow via red via blue to green. This sequence runs in a clockwise direction "with" the color circle; I have therefore called it–like all sequences of this direction–Con-Versions, as distinct from the Di-Versions of Figures 13-16.

206

9

13

10

14

205

11

15

12

16

Color Form Yellow

Diversion, 1970-1975, 1977
Nitrocellulose on phenolic resin plates
800 × 800 unframed

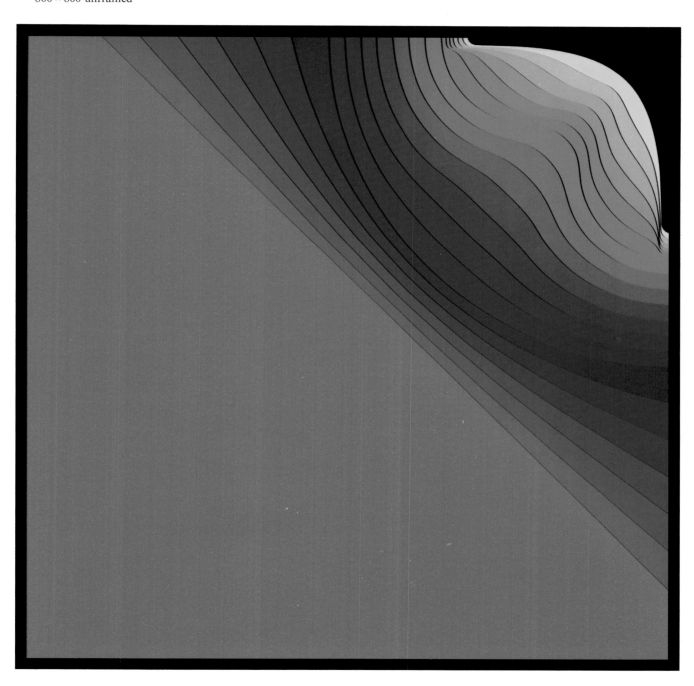

207

9. The Color Lines

A Preliminary Remark

This is the latest chapter–and at the same time one of the oldest. What I can say about it I have already said at length, in the booklet "Sketches for the Color Lines" (see page 214).

The Starting Point

More than twenty years ago I got to know the Basel mathematician Andreas Speiser. From the beginning he followed my work with sympathy and encouragement and let me share in his own interests: these were mainly concerned with the relationship between mathematics and art. Among other things he analyzed (geometric) ornamentation, particularly of Islamic art. I was fascinated.

In content these examples of ornament are meditation images of the greatest spiritual density. They are components of a culture which is self-contained and alien to us in its nature. In their formal aspect, however, they have a close affinity with modern constructive art. Was it possible to use the essence of their complexity and inventiveness for my own work?

The Idea

In order to explain what is involved I must first of all be allowed a parenthetical remark: Ornament is a formal domain. Where color is used (as I have said: in Islamic ornamentation for example), it is used topologically (see "The Color-Form Continuum," page 190). My idea was to use the color in the ornament typologically, that is to say to conceive color and form–more precisely, line–as a structural unit.

The Color Lines consist of a family of five colored lines, or linear colors. The family runs along the edge of the picture continuously in the sequence of its gradation. Toward the inside the individual lines depart from their parallelism and the colors from their gradation. In the center each color line forms an individual figure: all together they make a uniform whole in which each complements the other. The rule is: that there is neither a residue nor–although intersections are allowed–any overlapping.

The Color Lines are a mixture of chess, I Ching, and the glass pearl game. Besides the rule there are also typical phases of the game: phase 1 = opening; 2 = unfolding; 3 = projection; 4 = conclusion.

The Realization

Typical example: Color Lines C1/L9, page 211. The colors of the lines range from cobalt blue to dark gray. The intention is that the beholder should follow these colors like paths in a labyrinth; that he should experience the individuality of the separate figures, the way in which they simultaneously intersect and condition each other; that he should be receptive to the color interactions that appear, and their interplay of continuity and contrast. Ultimately, that the beholder should be stimulated to see in the Color Lines the innumerable pictures which are contained therein, "partly *actu*, partly *potentia*."

The lines of the Color Lines are plastic, triangular in cross section. Where two lines cross, one line does not pass over or under the other; instead they penetrate each other on the same plane.

The Beginnings

Although the Color Lines go back to my acquaintance with Andreas Speiser, it took some twenty years before I–after countless unsuccessful attempts–found the final (provisional?) form.

Exhibited for the first time in 1977, at Galerie 58, Rapperswil (illustrated on the invitation).

In 1978 Pablo Stähli published *Sketches for the Color Lines*, 24 facsimile pages from a sketchbook.

209

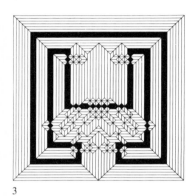

1

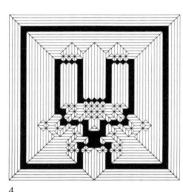

2

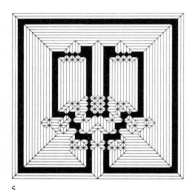

3

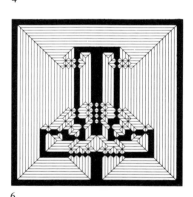

4

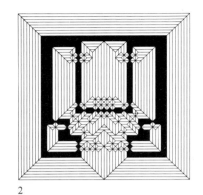

5

6

Color Lines C1/L9

Intro Version 1957, 1976-77
Nitrocellulose on wood
580 × 580 framed

All Color Lines consist of five figures, each with its own character and its individual expression, Figures 2 to 6. Superimposed on each other, these figures fill the pictorial space and leave no remainder; they fit together–in spite of their differences–to form a uniform whole.

The Color Lines can also be envisaged as a labyrinth where the eye can trace a path. Follow the paths in their intricate pattern and enjoy the interchange of the colors and the alternation of continuity and contrast.

(From the text accompanying an edition of the Volkswagenwerk, 1977)

211

Color Lines C13/L10

1976/1977
Extra Version
Nitrocellulose on wood
580 × 580 framed

212

Color Lines C15/L12

1976/1977
Intro Version
Nitrocellulose on wood
580 × 580 framed

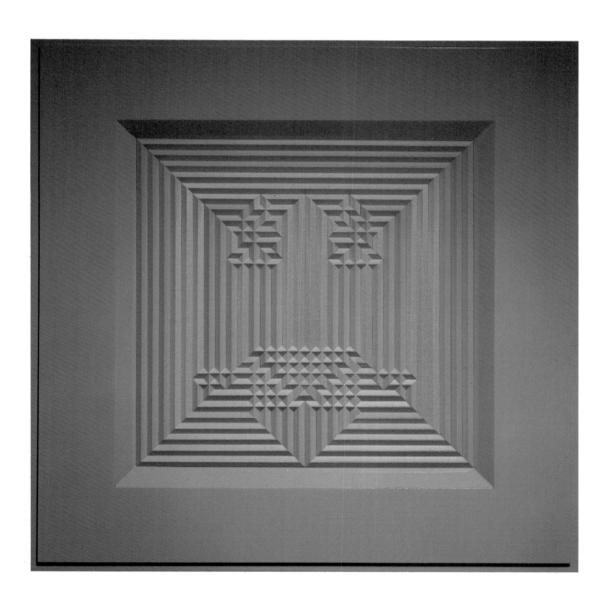

213

The Color Lines

**Reminiscences
of Andreas Speiser
instead of
coming to the point**

The Basel mathematician was one of the first–and certainly the most important–of those who took an interest in my serial pictures. Because of their geometric content, and even more because they displayed intimations of mathematical thinking. He was able to call my themes by their name and thus furnished me with conceptual instruments with which to work.

For example: from then onward a picture was no longer called composition XY but *The Large Sliding Mirror Picture*; another, *Cyclic Permutation*.

Or: to my attempts to express the serial element in my pictures by making it possible to change them in accordance with the law of sequence he added an unexpected historical dimension. He instructed me in Haydn's *Gioco harmonico*: a piece of 11×16 bars, from which–here a seventeen-digit figure would have to follow–sixteen-bar minuets can be produced. And this is done by aleatory combinations, the eleven alternatives available for each bar being decided by throwing dice.

* * *

Speiser was the most unprejudiced man I have ever known. The thing that was of interest to him in somebody was what interested him–otherwise, nothing.

For example: the expression in a face; how someone addressed the tram conductor. Then he might go through a whole tram and talk to people he didn't know from Adam: "My name is Speiser; who are you?" In the same way he made the acquaintance of Picasso; only in this case it was the pictures that interested him.

Or: I was standing near him one day when a Russian prince was introduced to him; a splendiferous name, an orotund title. Speiser's response was, "What do you do in life?"–was it worth wasting his attention on anything else? At a time when Le Corbusier was barely a name, let alone the architect of a house, Speiser plumped for him to be given an honorary doctorate of the University of Zurich. Le Corbusier's theories on the right angle and the Golden Section had been enough for Speiser to recognize his genius.

* * *

On meeting Speiser one had never to be surprised if he came to the point at once.

For instance, instead of asking "How are you?" he might say "Are you making the most of life?"

Or: conversely he surprised me by replying to my routine question about his health: "You know, I'm now old and gaga." I remember the incident very clearly: it was the last time I met him, shortly before his death. It was in front of the Museum of Fine Arts in Basel, which he–professor emeritus–visited almost every day. He said it without a trace of affectation, by the way, and I was to recall it afterward and not for that reason alone.

* * *

He had arranged to meet a student there and invited me to join them, for an original Speiser-conducted tour.

For instance, he explained the painting *Adam and Eve* by Holbein the Younger. One can see with half an eye that the apple is worm-eaten. Much more subtle was the way, he said, that Holbein had painted Adam's eyes. Two interpretations were possible. At one moment they look concupiscently at Eve; and at another they look up to heaven with, so to speak, a shrug. As if they wanted to say: you'll be astonished at the consequences of what I do.

Or: concerning a painting attributed to the school of Leonardo, Speiser asked: "What do you see? A man? A woman?" A moment's hesitation; the label says "Shepherd;" he wears his hair long. Speiser takes advantage of the pause: "You see, you don't see what it is. It is neither a man nor a woman; it is a hermaphrodite." He is cut off below the navel. Speiser suggested: he is not standing, he is hovering, the hermaphrodite is an angel. Nor is it a picture from Leonardo's school but by Leonardo himself. Proof: "Look at the foreshortening of the upper arm stretched toward the observer. That's a problem in mathematics and geometry and could only have been mastered by Leonardo himself at the time the picture was painted." (Incidentally I discovered later that books have already been written about this picture. In Basel there were two parties; Speiser belonged to the party that believed the picture was authentic. The student, by the way, was Bernd Völkle).

* * *

Speiser's education was as conventional as his behavior was unconventional: classical/universal; the humus on which he grew his pumpkins. The most colorful were thriving hybrids of mathematics and art.

For example, he discovered something about a gateway in the cloister of Basel Cathedral which–very likely–a stone mason had put there as a private joke. Looking at the base plans of the piers to left and right, one sees that the outlines are not only–as is usual–mirror images of each other but are also the wrong way round from outside inward in their lengths: what is long on the left is short on the right–and yet the flutings in the pointed arches run together as if there were no mystery at their base.

Or: in the paintings in the dome of Parma Cathedral by Correggio. Christ's ascension can–as Speiser showed–be experienced in reality, by the observer who knows what to do. If, starting at the entrance, one moves forward in the interior and looks up at the dome, one sees first of all its lower part: two or three disciples and the figure of Christ, which has only risen a few meters above the earth. As one moves forward, with gaze steadily directed at Christ, he rises visibly into the air. And on arriving under the dome, one sees Christ in heaven above blessing the congregation.

* * *

Speiser loved to confound one with monumental axioms, which forced one to think.

For example: there is no Nature. A tree is only a tree when a poet has seen it, when he has become aware of it, and when he has described it. There have been landscapes only since Petrarch created them in poetry–he climbed to the summit of Mont Ventoux and was overwhelmed by the panorama of the landscape.

Or: there is no such thing as feeling. How is that? Feeling is only ossified intellect; thinking which has become mere habit. Works of art created with feeling and imagination are, when examined more closely, nothing other than the application of acquired schemata. It is only in the mental world of the understanding that artistic work is possible. But the understanding is not an end in itself; it can only bring us to the edge of the world of intellect and spirit–the *mundus intelligibilis*. To catch a glimpse of the inside requires patience and good fortune. In the last analysis the creation of new forms is a mystery.

* * *

Mathematische Denkweise (Mathematical Thinking) is the title of one of his books; it was also the key-word of his life. For him it betokened a higher insight into the essence of all things. We are constantly receiving sensations, he said. But unless we bring our sensations into consciousness, unless we perpetuate them in formulae which are of general validity, everything is scattered by the wind. Thinking like this became with him a mental attitude which he applied to both the trivial and the important things of life.

To eating, for instance. Legend has it that he dined every Friday evening at the Odéon, Basel's leading restaurant at the time. Speiser is said to have composed his menu like a piece of music on the principle of prelude and fugue and to have celebrated his dinner with due solemnity. He used the same formulae for his *Anleitung zum inhaltlichen Denken* (Introduction to Intuitive Thinking).

Or: In his address as rector (at the University of Basel) he spoke of money. "All order comes from the greatest gift ever made to the understanding, that of number. Money is one of its highest and most important manifestations." Money must be given a high position. Like water. So that on its way down the valley it drives as many mills as possible. From money Speiser passed to freedom: "Freedom comes into being only through awareness as man understands and thinks about the connection between law and lawlessness. It does not originate from contingency but from higher regions, from understanding and reflection. One is freed from the bonds of Nature by studying its laws, and new freedom is created by formulating new laws. The recognition and thinking out of laws until complete clarity prevails and the decision that then ensues are the habitat of freedom."

* * *

It was Speiser's secret dream to see mathematics not merely as an aid to art. In a deceptively commonplace sentence he revealed his mind: "Perhaps it will be possible one day to demonstrate the power of mathematical thinking to create art."

For instance, with reference to Klein's circle figure, Speiser thought that if it could be based on a hexagon, it could be made into the plan of a cathedral. The whole point is a new spatial experience: in the "side chapels" one would be both alone and united with the whole interior. No doubt about it: the perspective thus obtained would be excitingly modern, but do we need cathedrals today? Unruffled, Speiser retorted: If not, then we should think of building a department store on the same plan. That we should certainly need. Later I discovered the Klein circle figure in Escher. Speiser subsequently condensed his obsession into a piece of jewelry: he had a brooch made for his wife in colored enamel.

Or: ornamentation from all periods of civilization–in which context, clearly, mathematics did not engender art but art mathematics. Speiser first of all analyzed ornaments from ancient Egypt and found that he could not grasp their complexity with any known mathematics. So he developed a new group theory for the purpose.

218

* * *

Speiser kindly allowed me to share in his interests. He transmitted his fascination for the Klein circle figure to me; but apart from my wonderment at the phenomenon, nothing of it remained lodged in my mind.

It was different with ornamentation, particularly the Islamic, the geometric more especially. This made an immediate impact on me and I knew that I would one day have to take up the theme. Here was a concept with a noble plenitude of spirit–nobler than the intellectually kindred realizations of constructive art–and it was this that moved me most of all. A great deal of what I have tried to show in my pictures was anticipated here.

And so it is to Andreas Speiser that I owe my thanks for the inspiration that led to the Color Lines–and for many, many other things. I have therefore taken this circuitous route via his personality–by way of homage and late thanks–to come to the matter in hand.

A pattern of Islamic ornament consists of a set of polygons which is turned, reflected, and displaced. Through its multifold intersections simple symmetries take shape. At first sight the observer sees figures –squares, stars, and the like–which appear to be completely regular in themselves and in their arrangement. On closer examination he realizes that all these figures are made by a single line which runs through the entire surface –following, as it seemed to me, fantastic courses.

Later, using photographs, I myself made analyses–not as a mathematician (I have no gift at all in that direction) but as an artist. In so doing, I discovered even more complex systems: groups of lines which–each independently–went their own ways but all formed coherent symmetries by being placed under and over each other, led through each other, and woven into each other.

* * *

And I also obtained new insights from another friend: from Henri Stierlin. He made it clear to me that the world of Islamic ornament is a self-contained one which is permeated through and through by the religion and philosophy of Islam. Therefore: it cannot be readily transposed to our occidental present.

Years later I visited the Alhambra near Granada. One of the most wonderful places man has created on this earth because everything here is human: the scale; the proportions; the interplay of concept and material; the setting of space and silence. Everything is atmosphere, condensed to unreality; where it is densest are ornaments.

I found this most clearly in the Hall of the Ambassadors. I imagined myself as an ambassador to the caliph sitting in one of the niches on soft cushions. I would smoke a hookah and let the ornament which, when one is seated, is at eye-level, work upon me. But of course, I was a tourist like everyone else. With my eyes I followed the lines and usually lost them after the third or fourth turn. But I began to have some idea of the high complexity the perception must develop if it is to absorb all this so that perfect clarity is attained. And, depending on my mood, I would take and absorb one of the thousand and one pictures which are contained in the ornament, partly in *actu* and partly in *potentia*.

* * *

The art of the arabesque is like a palimpsest. On the surface everything looks superficial, banal, taken for granted. I can accept the ornament for what its name indicates as adornment, as decoration. But as I peel away

**A glimpse into
the world of arabesques
–instead of
coming to the point**

layer after layer, more and more, spiritual dimensions come to view. Again this is an aspect found only in great art.

* * *

After I had completed the first series of Color Lines, I went to Isfahan; to have my work confirmed, so to speak.

If the Gothic cathedral represents the City of God aglow with light, the Persian mosque is the mirror of paradise: with its courtyard as an enclosed paradisial garden covered by the vault of heaven; in the center the pool with the eternally still water which purifies and gives life; on the four sides the iwams as cool grottos which are like stalactites; with the great dome which marks out the spiritual living space of the Muslims where they pray, sleep, talk to each other, and have their being–as if they were enjoying a foretaste of paradise here below.

One has to imagine oneself in a land of stony waste where the paradise of the mosques appears in cool colors; the tones passing from yellow through green to ultramarine; turquoise is dominant. And one must also imagine that these colors articulate themselves continuously into ornament. That it forms a part of the architecture, accompanies it, underlines it, or stands as a foil to it–in every case intensifying it, depending on the effect intended.

The ornament creates the impression that one is standing inside a cosmic-molecular structure; Nature is being experienced from inside. Actually, some Islamic ornament is identical with the atomic structures of natural substances which modern science has only just discovered. (This brings me back to Speiser, who showed that the tower of Strasbourg Cathedral corresponds to the crystalline structure of graphite).

* * *

We are accustomed to distinguishing between things analytically, to conceiving them in terms of the law of cause and effect; the limits of our thinking are called space and time. In Islam the law of the eternal present prevails; the correspondence of everything with everything; the unity of space and time, of cause and effect. And nowhere does this law find better expression than in the art of ornament, and nowhere more magnificently than at Isfahan.

(From Sketches for the Color Lines, *24 Facsimile Pages from a Sketchbook, Editions Pablo Stähli, Zurich, 1978.)*

220

Editor's Postscript

To bring a book into being is an adventure: intellectually and materially. A book on art–particularly a book on contemporary art like this one–is also a personal adventure, for it involves an exchange of ideas between the author and the editor.

Out of the dangers confronted together emerges a form of complicity, and out of this a friendship, or in the case of Karl Gerstner and myself, a deepening of friendship. Our collaboration afforded me an opportunity to discover the most hidden secrets of his mind, the structures of his thinking, and the consequences of its implementation. It allowed me not only to improve my acquaintance with an œuvre and an artist: it also gave me an insight into a human being who lives in perfect harmony with what he creates. I mention this at the outset because such cases are extremely rare.

* * *

It will soon be 25 years since we first met. I was art critic on a daily paper when, in 1957, I was given a small book to review. It was a slim volume, yet at the same time how dense and rich! The title was *Cold Art?*, and the unknown author was Karl Gerstner. It seemed to me to be of astonishing and resolute originality. And its uncompromising rigor fascinated me. In it the author described the roots of an art–his art–that was so new that most people asked themselves: can that still be art?

The thread of Gerstner's thinking started with the pioneer generations, with the Cubists and, after them, the painters of De Stijl. In a second chapter he then spun this thread over the painters of the middle generation, the representatives of concrete art. He was the first to analyze some of their most prominent works in order to reveal the principles they held in common: the picture plane as the real and ideal starting point, its individualization first by division into logically structured fields and second by the accentuation of these fields with colors. Their common aim was, in fact, to confer on this picture plane its autonomy as a work of art–in its intellectual conception and its sensual perception. Gerstner drew its artistic genealogy, in which names like Vantongerloo, Albers, Lohse, and Bill form an uninterrupted line of artists with whom he feels elective affinities.

The third chapter–the young generation–was linked up to points in the future which long ago became the present. In this connection he provided the theoretical superstructure for a continued development of concrete art that was as bold as it was creative and subsequently expanded and deepened it in contributions to the periodical *Spirale*, which–excellently designed and published by Eugen Gomringer, Diter Rot, and Marcel Wyss–had the character of a manifesto for the new art. Many of his contributions to *Spirale* have been included in this book.

A few weeks after the appearance of my enthusiastic review of *Cold Art?* we met in Basel.

I saw Gerstner's work for the first time in the original–and I must admit: it came as a great shock. Most of the pictures were in gray, black, and white, coldly and perfectly executed; they consisted of magnetized strips whose position could be changed, or of eccentric circles which could be turned on themselves in such a way that one could create one's own pictures to taste. The pictures were so devised that collaboration between the artist and his public came about, as it were, automatically.

But the shock was exceeded by my surprise on finding that the artist who had created these works, with their "mechanical" and "calculated" aspect, was a warm-hearted individual, open and deep-feeling, a person who–unlike his works–was in no way severe but capable of enthusiasm and fond of laughter. But the contrast between the work and the person was only apparent. The novelty of expression, the violent break with tradition, the partisanship for the absolute could only be the manifestation of a vigorous temperament, a temperament with communicative élan, and a strong determination to persuade. At the time, incidentally, Gerstner was also working on the reform of graphic design and typography, an activity which–however successful–was in his eyes always bound up with his art and subordinate to it.

* * *

In this early period he took the idea of the "serial," which his friend Paul Gredinger had coined for electronic music, and transferred it to his painting. This step found its most conspicuous expression in the color series, which Karl Gerstner introduced into modern art; a fact, incidentally, which is not widely known but to which Max Bill paid tribute a few years ago in a speech at an exhibition of Karl Gerstner's works: "Gerstner is probably the first to take up this method again. Today there are others who pride themselves greatly on having done this before and yet they can adduce no evidence if it should be called for." The principle of the color series, which was first used only in the range of white, gray, and black, was then extended step by step to all colors of the visible spectrum in a resonant and grandiose universe.

Gerstner's method of creating a system in terra incognita and then applying it to complete his explorations was consistent with my own thinking as an art historian–whether I was concerned with the rhythmic forms in the ornamentation of Maya architecture or the geometrical structures of Islamic mosaics, to name two examples. It was to find its purest expression in *The Spirit of Colors*, in which the author elaborates principles which again and again–by feedback as it were–are modulated and deepened in his pictures.

For between theory and practice there is interaction and agreement: the creative act and the step to realization which follows it and at the same time calls it in question. The passage of time has revealed a secret to me, namely: Gerstner does not write his texts for, say, pedagogic reasons and, indeed, not even to communicate this thought; rather, they are method; they form a kind of inspirational technique for his personal use. He considers writing to be the most binding way of thinking back over a work and forward to the next one.

Since grasping this, I have realized that the Gerstnerian way of exploring, in which progress along the paths of art achieved by creative means runs parallel to the "philosophical" statement, offers itself not only as a book *on* a subject but also as the subject itself. In other words: Gerstner's work had perforce to lead to this publication, which is, in a way, the synthesis of a process fed by various contributions in the form of articles and essays which have appeared over the years, scattered in unconnected fragments in many periodicals and exhibition catalogs.

* * *

The idea for this book goes back some seven or eight years. It took a long time to prepare, mainly because of the joint efforts required to fuse the immense mass of "pictures" and "essays" into a strictly ordered but organic totality. One of the consequences of this was that Gerstner worked over all the theoretical studies collected here. Without altering the contents he has worked indefatigably to enrich them and to give his utterances greater precision. It is these efforts that give their formulation a very personal style and also make them more readily accessible to the reader who comes to the subject with no specific background but is interested in it.

The central theme is "the precision of sensation;" the medium is color which ever and again he supplies, interprets, and reflects on.

* * *

The initial plan was that the book should consist of two parts, "essays" and "pictures". However, it soon became clear that the two parts are complementary, and where they are complementary, they must run parallel without break or interruption. The result is this work which is neither monograph nor theory but something homogeneous and original.

* * *

It was the great retrospective which André Kamber organized in the Museum of Fine Arts in Solothurn in 1978 which provided the final impetus and resulted in Gerstner's oeuvre being finally organized, in nine chapters of pictures which are defined partly thematically and partly chronologically.

The Spirit of Colors contains not only texts already published elsewhere; "The Color-Form Continuum," which is the fruit of many years of research, is presented for the first time. It is, as it were, the crowning point of Karl Gerstner's work; he uses it to tie together his speculations into a coherent whole, a closed but dynamic system, an artistic and intellectual unit; a fundamental reference for a system of order both sensitive and mathematical in which perception and comprehension of the work come close together.

May this book reflect the enthusiasm which has presided over its creation. And may all who are fascinated by the adventure of contemporary art derive from it a new vision of the mystery of color. At all events it provides the key in the search for this aesthetic world to which Karl Gerstner is committed. And besides being a thing of beauty, a reflection of a powerful oeuvre, the book should also be a useful instrument; it should help to decipher the message of color and hence that of a pure art.

* * *

I myself see the book (not without pride) as a confirmation of what I wrote–almost 25 years ago–in my first article: this is an artist who will have to be reckoned with.

Henri Stierlin

DATE DUE	